A Search for What Is Real

Finding Faith

Zondervan Books by Brian D. McLaren

Brian D. McLaren
Foreword by Steve Chalke

A Search for
What Is Real

Finding Faith

ZONDERVAN®

ZONDERVAN.com/
AUTHORTRACKER
follow your favorite authors

We want to hear from you. Please send your comments about this book to us in care of zreview@zondervan.com. Thank you.

ZONDERVAN®

Finding Faith — A Search for What Is Real
Copyright © 1999, 2007 by Brian D. McLaren

Previously published as parts 3–5 of *Finding Faith:
A Self-Discovery Guide for Your Spiritual Quest*

Requests for information should be addressed to:

Zondervan, *Grand Rapids, Michigan 49530*

Library of Congress Cataloging-in-Publication Data

McLaren, Brian D., 1956–
    Finding faith : a search for what makes sense / Brian D. McLaren.
    p. cm.
    Includes bibliographical references.
    ISBN–10: 0-310-27267-X (softcover)
    ISBN–13: 978-0-310-27267-0 (softcover)
    1. Spirituality. 2. Faith 3. Apologetics. I. Title.
BV4501.3.M372 2006
230—dc22   2006034755

Interior design by Michelle Espinoza

Printed in the United States of America

---

06 07 08 09 10 11 12 • 20 19 18 17 16 15 14 13 12 11 10 9 8 7 6 5 4 3 2 1

This book is dedicated to all who are seeking faith, spirituality, purpose, hope, and God. The fact that you care enough to seek means that you have already found more than you may know.

Contents

Foreword

A man once dreamt of leaving his home to go in search of the Eternal City, which lay on the other side of a vast forest. No one in his town had ever been there, but the stories about its size and beauty had been told for generations. Eventually the desire to go and see this wonderful place for himself became overwhelming. So one morning the man woke early and, after saying goodbye to his wife and young child, set out on his journey of discovery.

The man traveled for many hours, trekking through the forest that separated his own town from the Eternal City, stopping only to take refreshments and eat the simple meal he had taken with him. He had no idea how long his journey would take or what he would actually find at its end, but his determination was constantly fueled by the inspirational stories of his intended destination. Eventually, however, despite his great enthusiasm for the journey ahead of him, he became exhausted. Finding a clearing, he settled down under the boughs of a large tree to rest.

Not wanting to awake disoriented and so lose the direction he was traveling, the man took off his shoes and laid them side-by-side with them pointing along the path he was taking. Assured that he would now not get lost, he closed his eyes and fell into a deep sleep.

While he slept, two boys out playing in the forest entered the clearing and stumbled across him. Seeing the man asleep, they decided to play a trick on him. As silently as possible they crept closer and closer to him with the intent of hiding his shoes, but just as one of the boys had them in his grasp, the man began to stir. Startled, the boy dropped the shoes and fled with his companion into the cover of the forest. The man sat up and stared around with blurry eyes, but saw nothing. Convinced it was nothing more than a forest animal, he fell back to sleep.

The following morning the man rose from his slumber, and carefully putting on his shoes so that they continued to point in the direction of the Eternal City, he set off once more in search of it. He walked for the whole day until finally, as dusk fell, he came to the edge of the forest—and there before his eyes was the Eternal City. It didn't look particularly special, nor did it seem much bigger than the small town he had left. But he had come this far, so he approached its perimeter wall. As he got closer, he realized how similar it looked to the home he had left. He walked down what felt like familiar roads, past familiar shops and houses. Eventually he came across a familiar street, where he found a familiar house. He knocked on a familiar door and was greeted by the wife and child he had left behind to go in search of the Eternal City.

"The real voyage of discovery consists not in seeking new lands, but seeing with new eyes," wrote Marcel Proust.

A scientist may, on being kissed by her husband before she leaves for work in the morning, describe the experience as the outcome of "neck-muscle movements reducing the distance between two pairs of lips, a reciprocal transmission of carbon dioxide and microbes, and a contraction of orbicular muscles" (so writes David Wilkinson in his book *The Message of Creation: Encountering the Lord of the Universe*). And at one level this would be an extremely accurate assessment of the exchange.

But at the same time, her explanation would be nothing if not woefully inadequate—for, in truth, the kiss was the outcome and demonstration of love.

There is more, far more, to life than can be measured empirically—by physical touch and observation. Science might be able to analyze Leonardo's *Mona Lisa* and tell us how he painted it: what kind of paints he used, what colors he had on his palette, how he changed it as he went, even which part of the canvas he painted on first. But what it can never explain is why he painted what he painted in the first place. What were the emotions that stirred him to paint; what inspired him to complete his task rather than give up? And science certainly cannot answer the riddle of Mona Lisa's curious smile.

In this book—which, as you will discover, is a companion to *Finding Faith—A Search for What Makes Sense*, Brian McLaren seeks to address the mystery of faith at exactly this level. That companion volume is, as Brian puts it, "for people seeking a faith that makes intellectual sense" whereas the pages that follow are for those of us who are searching for a faith we "can feel" and who intuitively know that in doing so we are actually "seeking for something beyond faith itself: we are seeking truth, love, purpose, and a sense of place in the universe."

"I won't pretend to have no beliefs myself—that would be dishonest. Instead, I will try to be open about my own conclusions without imposing them on you," Brian writes. "My goal," he explains, "is to help you discover how to believe—how to search for and find a faith that is real, honest, good, enriching, and yours."

A few months ago I sat in a restaurant with a good friend of mine who has been struggling with questions of faith for some years. "I can't do all this stuff," he complained to me. "I can't get my head around it." In response I asked him this question: "If you could discover what it is that God is doing and then join in, would you be interested?" He paused, he thought, he smiled, and then gently he replied, "Of course."

I commend this book to all who restlessly seek to see life with new eyes.

Steve Chalke, MBE
Founder of Oasis Global,
Faithworks, and www.Church.co.uk

Introduction

Just about everybody has seen the classic film *The Wizard of Oz*. Sometimes when I am teaching, I play a little game based on the film. I will begin a line from the film and see if people can complete it. For example, I might say ...

> I'll get you, my pretty, and ...
> There's no place ...
> That's a horse of ...
> We're not in ...
> Well, bust my ...
> Somewhere, over ...

In each case, people can finish the line. What is it about this 1939 movie that still captures our imagination so many years later? In part, I think, it is the resonance we feel with the story of a search. The tin man is searching for a heart, the lion for courage, the scarecrow for a brain, and Dorothy for home. All of us, I think, resonate with the realization that something is missing in our lives. We are all, to one degree or another, tin men, scarecrows, cowardly lions, and dislocated runaways. The modern world is truly an Oz—an amazing Technicolor place—but something in us feels displaced, disheartened, discouraged, and even deranged (by which I mean knocked out of our normal range). We are not fully at home, and we are looking for a band of friends with whom we can go on a quest to find what is missing.

The film serves, I think, as a metaphor for the search for faith. As tin men, we need to reconnect with the intuitive part of our beings, the part of us sensitive to goodness and beauty, to love and meaning, the part of us that can't be reduced to a mechanism. As scarecrows, we are smart enough to realize our stupidity, but not smart enough to do anything about it. As individuals and as societies and civilizations, we know we are living at an unsustainable pace, turning the human race into a rat race, reducing ourselves to consumers, destroying our environment in a sprint toward a finish line that we haven't even chosen. We think we can overcome violence with violence, hatred with hatred, vengeance with revenge, greed with greed—even though it hasn't worked so far, we keep doing the same things hoping for different results. Like the proverbial addict, we think more of what's destroying us will finally make us happy—another drink of prosperity, another dose of power, another shot of pleasure, another bottle of bigger/faster/more, another hit of hurry. We are stuck on a nail, paralyzed like the scarecrow in the cornfield, and we are just wise enough to know we lack wisdom.

Like the cowardly lion, we know we lack the "verve and nerve" to face our challenges. We put on a good show, but we know we are in part at least a big fraud. And like Dorothy, we ran away from our true home, but then got into a tornado of trouble we hadn't bargained for. We are not sure where we are, and in our dislocation and derangement, we want somehow to get back to our proper location, our home "range." Put this need together—for heart, for wisdom, for courage, and for home—and you have defined the need that becomes a calling, a vocation, a quest: the search for faith.

But this search isn't easy. There is a quiet, background voice of skepticism in our world that tells us faith is primitive, stupid, uneducated, unintellectual, unscientific, unenlightened, an anachronism, an evolutionary appendix that we need to outgrow and leave behind. Can you have faith and still have a brain, or does faith exclude wisdom-seeking scarecrows, requiring them to leave whatever brains they have at the door? If you move away from the voice of the skeptics and approach many religious communities, you too often find a kind of heartless, programmed, mechanical ritualism—a round of services and activities and duties that seem devoid of meaning and low in impact. Or else you find a kind of angry, grim, elitist, controlling judgmentalism—devoid of heart by being devoid of compassion. Tin men seeking a heart won't be welcome in either ritualist or judgmentalist settings. And lions seeking courage easily find themselves discouraged by the domesticating influences of both secular and religious communities. They conspire to turn us into rats in a maze, hamsters on a wheel, or sheep in a fold, not lions roaring with courage.

If these dissatisfactions resonate with you, if you feel compelled to seek something more, then we have a lot in common. I have been a seeker since my teenage years, maybe even before. My search has led me to be a person of faith. Now to say I have faith is interesting, because part of me says, no, I don't possess it—I am still seeking it. Whenever I think I have it, whatever I have feels like a tiny seed, a tiny drop, a tiny spark. I grasp it, but when I open my hand to look at it or measure it, there is nothing there.

But then I realize that many possessions, perhaps all possessions are, paradoxically, like this: having them isn't the point, because having them is about wanting something else. I have a car, for example, not because I want a car, but because I want to get places I am not currently in. The possession of the car is meaningful because it helps me go on a journey. I don't really want a car: I want mobility. Similarly, I have a computer, not because I want a computer, but because I want to send and receive emails, write books and articles, explore cyberspace. The possession of the computer is meaningful because it helps me seek, pursue, explore. I own so many books because I am seeking knowledge, understanding, stimulation for my mind and imagination, and the books that line my shelves help me in my pursuit of what I seek. Finally, I own a home. Why? Not because I want wood and aluminum and plumbing and paint, but because I am seeking love and belonging and connection to my wife, my kids, my neighbors and friends. The home I have helps me in my quest for these precious things that I seek.

"Having" faith is like "having" a home or a car or a computer. Having faith is really about seeking something beyond faith itself: we are seeking truth, love, purpose, and a sense of place in the universe, which is what the scarecrow, tin man, cowardly lion, and displaced teenager are really seeking in *The Wizard of Oz*. If we believe that truth, love, purpose, and connection are realities which are ultimately found in God, then really, both the film — and the book you are now holding — are about something beyond the search for faith: they are about the search for God. Faith is simply a means to that end.

When I originally began writing this book, I wanted to provide comprehensive help for people in this search, help that I wish had been there for me. The result was a book over three hundred pages long. Eventually my publisher and I realized that a book of that length might intimidate many of the people we hoped it would help, so we decided to make two books. The first book, in a sense, would primarily serve scarecrows (or the scarecrow in each of us). It would be for people seeking a faith that makes intellectual sense. This second book would aim to serve tin men and cowardly lions (or those parts of each of us). It would be for people seeking a faith they can feel. Together, they would help people seeking to find their place in the big scheme of things. If you are seeking for a faith you have never had, trying to recover a faith you lost, or trying to hold onto a faith that seems to be slipping through your fingers, we hope both books will be helpful to you.

In both books, instead of trying to tell you "the answers" via dogmatic pronouncements (as many well-meaning people have already tried to do for you, no doubt), I would like to try to help you find the answers yourself. Instead of trying to tell you what to believe or focusing on why you should believe, my goal is to help you discover how to believe — how to search for and find a faith that is real, honest, good, enriching, transforming, and yours.

Good Questions and True Stories

This goal will require an approach that focuses more on questions than answers. My job will be to lead you to and through important questions, in a sensible order, since good questions are among the most important tools for a good quest. While some questions tend to lead to dead ends or vicious circles of controversy, other questions, approached in a sensible order, can help a person progress in his or her search at a good pace, not rushing, but not wasting time either. Rather than presenting one answer only — what I might feel is the "right" answer — I will try to guide you through each of the more plausible answers and encourage you to make your own choices. Again, I won't pretend to have no beliefs myself, which would be dishonest. Instead, I will try to be open about my own conclusions without imposing them on you. You may agree with me; you may not. I will feel I have been of some service to you either way simply by stimulating your thinking.

Along with questions, I have found that stories can be of great help in the search, so you will find many true stories — my own and others' — included in each chapter. (As you would expect, I have changed some names and details to avoid invading anyone's privacy.) One of my main credentials as a pastor is that I myself have had most of the doubts or spiritual problems anyone else has ever come to me with, so I hope the accounts of my struggles will offer you something to identify with and learn from too.

In *Finding Faith — A Search for What Makes Sense*, we explored a series of intellectual questions:

1. Does It Really Matter What I Believe?
2. What Is the Relationship Between Faith and Knowledge?
3. How Does Faith Grow?
4. Can I Believe in Atheism?
5. Is "I Don't Know" All I Need to Know?
6. If There Is One God, Why Are There So Many Religions?
7. Do You Seriously Expect Me to Think of God As an Old Man with a Long White Beard?
8. Don't All Paths Lead to the Same God?

If those questions are of interest to you, I hope you will read that book. In this book, however, we will explore more experiential questions, as you will see in the table of contents and chapter previews. At the end of each chapter you will find a section called Your Response, which can be used in two ways. First, if you write your responses, you will compose a kind of personal creed, which can help you in your spiritual journey. Second, if you use these questions for dialogue with some friends, you can enjoy one of life's greatest pleasures — people talking openly about life's deepest matters. Following the response section, you will find recommended resources (books, tapes, videos, websites, and more) and finally, sample prayers, which can help you express and exercise your faith as it grows.

I am writing not as a preacher (though sometimes I do preach) and certainly not as a scholar, but as a friend and fellow seeker. In that light, let's imagine we are having a cup of coffee together or taking a walk on a riverside trail. Let's imagine you asked me a question like this: *Brian, I am just getting started in my spiritual search. How can a person like me experience God?*

Part 1

Spiritual
Experience

How Might I Experience God?

This chapter introduces five of twelve ways in which people commonly experience God: ritual, nature, obedience, worship, and community. It includes a number of stories that illustrate each means of experiencing God.

Who Should Read This Chapter?

If you are interested in actually experiencing God in some way, chapters 1 and 2 will be very important for you.

What Questions Does It Address?

How can God be experienced through ritual? Why should we expect to find God through nature? How does doing what you don't necessarily want to help you experience God? Why is worship more appropriate than analysis for experiencing God? Why is involvement with other people important in experiencing God?

The birds ... became a key whereby I might unlock eternal things.

Roger Tory Peterson, author of
A Field Guide to the Birds

I say that this search for God was born not of reason but of an emotion because it was a search that arose not from my thought process—indeed, it was in direct opposition to my thinking—but from my heart. It was a feeling of dread, of loneliness, of forlornness in the midst of all that was alien to me; and it was a feeling of hope for someone's help.

Leo Tolstoy, *A Confession*

1

How Might I Experience God?

Many of us need to grapple with a list of important intellectual questions before we can seek faith. Those questions are like obstacles in the road that must be cleared; we can't pretend they are not there and we cannot avoid dealing with them. Others of us, though, assume from the beginning that we will never "fit God into our heads," and so we set another goal — to try to get our heads, and hearts, "into God." In other words, it makes sense to us that we will experience our way into God before we think our way to God, if we are ever going to get connected to God at all. Even those of us (like me) who must grapple with intellectual questions (the kind we address in *Finding Faith — A Search for What Makes Sense*) often reach a point where we say, "Yes, I believe I can find answers to my questions that will make some sort of honest faith in God possible. But what will push me from believing faith is possible in general to actually believing something in particular?" The conclusion we usually make is that some sort of spiritual experience would be helpful in our quest.

But what do we do? Go sit under a tree somewhere until enlightenment falls upon us like an apple? That's possible for some people, I suppose, but if you have diapers to change, bills to pay, contracts to sign, soccer games to attend, kitchens to clean, patients to see, or other normal daily responsibilities, the "sit under a tree" approach seems rather exclusive. As an alternative, perhaps we should just put the burden of proof on God: if God wants us to believe in her, him, or it, God will need to get our attention somehow. Until then, we will continue as agnostics or atheists or whatever. Sometimes we place the burden of proof on God because trying to figure out how to find God seems overwhelming, but that approach seems rather passive. Where, then, do we start? How do we know how to begin?

Fortunately, human beings have been trying to connect to God for thousands of years, and their experiences can teach us much about what people have done through the centuries to make themselves susceptible to the experience of God. Not only that, but when certain ways of experiencing God are fine-tuned through the ages, we have reason to believe they have more value than a random shot in the dark or a passive "see what happens" approach.

Before we look at a dozen or so common ways of experiencing God (starting with five in this chapter), it would help to define what we mean by the term *experience*, but that won't be easy. For example, people with severe mental illnesses often experience hallucinations, and those experiences seem very real, but we are seeking something more than that. Perhaps we could say we are seeking a *true* experience, but how do we know that our experiences are true? After all, people often experience falling in love — *true* love, they call it — and they experience intense ecstasy in the company of a person who later turns out to be a jerk. Looking back, they feel the experience of true love blinded them to reality instead of helping them touch reality.

This is our dilemma. We want and need experience, something we feel, something that happens to us, something that goes beyond ideas or arguments. But we can't trust experience alone;

we must test our experience rationally so we are not deceived by it. But if rationality is always debunking or disqualifying our experience, we feel we are locked in a box and we are missing important facets of life.

Western culture over the last five hundred years or so has struggled with this dilemma. An argument has simmered between rationalists and romantics. Rationalists thought that cold reason, objective observation, and impersonal logic ("Just the facts, Ma'am") were the best way to discover truth. Experiences, emotions, mysticism, intuition and the like were suspect. Romantics felt just the opposite. "Follow your heart," they would say. In situations like these, where you have two packs of dogs barking up two different trees, I am more prone to say that there is something interesting up both trees. I suppose you could say that *Finding Faith — A Search for What Makes Sense* is geared more toward rationalists, and this book more toward romantics. But recalling *The Wizard of Oz*, rationalists like the Tin Man want a heart, and romantics like the Scarecrow want a brain, and each gains something from the other, and each offers something to the other. So it makes sense to journey on together, believing that experience — feelings, intuitions, things that happen to us that move us toward faith — are indeed important, even though they are only part of the story.

I hope that sets the stage for us to survey ways that people commonly experience God in ways that give them a good faith, an honest faith, a life-transforming faith.

1. Nature/Creation

My wife and I have a lot in common, but in one way we are nearly opposites. Grace is a city girl, comfortable in shopping malls and on sidewalks between skyscrapers. I am more of an outdoors guy whose idea of a good time is a hike in the mountains or a walk through a swamp. It's no wonder that creation is extremely important to me in my experience of God, while my wife (so far, anyway) finds other avenues — like going to an art museum, having deep conversations with friends, or reading a book of theology — more valuable.

I must be honest. Even for me, sometimes creation doesn't "work" as a way of connecting with God. Sometimes I take a walk in the woods and the flowers are just flowers to me, the dirt just dirt, the sky just sky, the wind just wind. My thoughts are abuzz with worries like flies, and my mind and heart go blank like white noise. I could just as well be sitting in a bus station or fast food joint or the Department of Motor Vehicles. I am completely uninspired.

But there are other times when I feel that every bush could at any moment become a "burning bush," alive with the glory of God, that the next breeze could carry a "still, small voice" speaking to me of God's presence and love; that running water and singing birds can become God's voice, speaking to me of joy and comfort; that thunderheads can shake me and bathe me and charge me with the power and majesty of God. That is why I make it a habit to go into the woods and to walk by the streams often in hopes that, if I am open, today might be a day when each flower and leaf and bush are more than "just" anything, and like Moses in the old story, I will realize that I am on holy ground.

This experience of God through nature comes to me on many levels. There is an intellectual level. I ponder the amazing intricacy of an organism, its perfect "fitness" for its environment, or the amazing ways the elements of an environment work together to make a self-sustaining system. I think about the intricacy of the theory of evolution, of the expansion of the universe blooming out from a primordial big bang. I find myself saying, "God, what an amazing artist, engineer, scientist, inventor, manager, and risk-taker you are." The awe we feel when contemplating the intricacy of our own bodies (from our ability to leap and run, to the capacities of a strand of DNA) can be, in a real way, an experience of God. But there are dimensions that go beyond intellect too. One of the essential experiences of mysticism is an awareness of a glory hidden in all of creation, in every tree and blade of grass and speck of dust and grain of sand. That experience, I think, is an experience of the creator, coming through the medium of God's creation.

If you feel there is much more to say about this subject, I agree. That is why we will return to this theme in great detail in chapters 7 and 9. But perhaps you feel more like my wife: you just don't get this venue for experiencing God. You would prefer that your experiences of God be indoors, in civilization, if possible!

2. Ritual

Many people experience God more readily in a cathedral than a verdant forest. Religious ritual seems to do for them what outdoor enjoyment does for me. The familiarity and repetition of ritual become for them a kind of transparency, putting them in a frame of mind where the ritual acts and words themselves become invisible, creating a "field" or "space" where they experience God as real, near, present. In a similar way, perhaps, I find that when I really want to concentrate, I sometimes put on music or go sit in a fast-food restaurant with its noises and activity. In that unlikely setting, rather than being distracted, the act of shutting out the distractions can help me concentrate more fully than if I were alone in a quiet library. Somehow, being in the crowd helps me experience a special kind of solitude. Similarly, ritual creates space for solitude, concentration, and reflection for at least some of us; we put ourselves in a place with other people, where a lot is going on — stained glass, statues, music, words, candles, perhaps incense — but the place becomes conducive to our concentrating on God. The place of ritual becomes a portal into the experience of God.

Bonding to Meaning

I found this definition of ritual to be helpful: *ritual means using our bodies to bond to meaning.* There are two parts to a ritual, then: what we do with our bodies and the meaning that we bond to through our actions.

Now some of you are probably thinking, "But I hate ritual! It's what turned me off to religion and God. All that standing, sitting, reciting ... it meant nothing to me." When ritual turns people off in this way, usually it is because they are expected to do something with their bodies without agreeing with or even understanding, let alone experiencing, the meaning associated with it. We could call ritual action without bonding to meaning *ritualism.* But even if we haven't consciously understood or even articulated the meaning we are bonding to, sometimes the ritual works anyway. It seems to reach us on an unconscious level.

Think of dating, for example. Why do so many couples repeat the ritual of going to dinner together? Most have probably never even considered this question. If they were to think about it, they might realize that although the date is not only about physical eating, the eating *is* truly important. Yes, it provides a reason to sit still and talk for a while, but I think it is more than that. The act of eating and drinking evokes hunger, thirst, satisfaction, pleasure. It also suggests the safety and belonging of being in a family together. In a sense, then, even without realizing it, a couple on a date is relating physical hunger and thirst to their emotional and relational hunger and thirst—the desire to get to know each other. They are associating the physical pleasure of eating with the meaningful experience of "tasting" or "drinking in" one another's personality, stories, background, humor, ideas, feelings. And perhaps they are bonding to the possibility of being family together. Maybe they never have realized it, but their dating is an eating ritual where they bond to the meaning of being nourished and filled and satisfied by one another's company.

The dating ritual of going to the movies might work in a similar way: we rest together, we let our imaginations be carried away together, we laugh or experience fear or romance or adventure together. We sit, looking in the same direction, sharing an experience and entering a story we can talk about after the movie ends.

Now, consider the Jewish celebration of Passover. It is a kind of yearly date where a family shares a ritual meal, evoking a time in the distant past when their ancestors ate a meal in preparation for a long journey to freedom. As they taste each item of food on the table, they bond to a unique meaning. The Christian celebration of communion works the same way; in fact, it is an adaptation of the Passover meal. The ritual centers on eating a piece of bread and drinking a sip of wine, while pondering the words of Jesus: "This is my body, given for you ... this cup is the new covenant in my blood, which is poured out for you for the forgiveness of sins ... as often as you do this, do it in remembrance of me." Isn't it possible that the act of eating and drinking, in a meditative frame of mind, can help one actually nourish himself or herself on God? Couldn't a person be helped in her experience of God by saying—with or without specific words—something like this? "God, I want to take you into my soul just as this food and drink come into my body. Just as the bread becomes part of my substance, and just as the wine carries its bittersweet heat down deep within me.... I want you, God, to become part of my whole being."

Meanwhile, another person might also be experiencing God in a slightly different way, bonding to meaning like this: "Jesus said his blood was shed for the forgiveness of sins. I think now of my sins, my wrongs, my lust the other day, that lie I told my coworker, the anger I had toward my wife, my hurriedness with my kids.... As I eat this ritual meal, I bond to the story of Jesus' crucifixion. As his body was broken like this bread, as his blood was poured out like this wine, he was feeling the ugliness and pain of human evil, and somehow he took all human evil into the heart of God, so I could be forgiven. Just as I drink this wine, I drink in God's gracious forgiveness...." And at that same moment, another person nearby is praying, "God, I am bonding to the meaning of being part of your family, together with these people who I am bonding to as my brothers and sisters." And still another is recalling the stories of Jesus eating meals with people as a metaphor of his message of "the kingdom of God." Is it too hard to imagine how this one simple ritual could be means of experiencing God in a hundred different ways?

The Body, and Just Showing Up

Kneeling, fasting, feasting, bowing, singing, chanting, raising the hands, standing ... rituals of faith involve the body in many ways. I suppose preaching could be seen as a ritual too. Few people remember much in the way of specifics after they hear a sermon (I say this with some sadness, as a preacher myself!). But perhaps that's okay. Perhaps just putting oneself in a quiet place, where the topic of conversation and contemplation is not just how to get rich, how to lose weight, or how to be more popular or successful, but rather where the topic is God and the spiritual life ... perhaps just putting oneself in such a place puts one in a posture to experience God. It's a way of bonding to the meaning that God might in some way speak to me. Maybe it doesn't happen every week. Maybe it happens only one week a year. But most who have in any way experienced God would agree: the hope of that one "catch" makes all fifty-two "fishing trips" worthwhile.

Devotional Reading and Special Days

The same could be said for devotional reading, which is in a sense preaching to oneself. Reading works about the spiritual life, especially the Bible, has played an important part for millions of people in experiencing God. Today (as we will see in chapter 5), many people struggle with the Bible. It seems so foreign, so distant, and in many ways, so odd and even repulsively violent to many of us. My grandmother used to say, in her wonderful Scottish brogue, that the best way to read the Bible was like eating fish: *Concentrate on enjoying the meat, lad, and put the bones aside.* Later on, she implied, if there's still time and you're still hungry, you can go back and work on the bones, the things that bother or confuse you. Just taking the time to sit and read—or to join a Bible study class or discussion group—can be a kind of ritual through which we bond to the meaning that God may have something to say to us if we will put ourselves in a listening posture.

The observance of holy days, Sabbaths, and the like would also fit into this category of ritual. Again, the ritual of setting aside one day in seven for rest and the care of one's soul, for attending to one's search for God, for the nurturing of one's faith ... that can't help but put a person in an appropriate posture for experiencing God. But then again, there's no guarantee. One can go to church or synagogue or mosque for all the wrong reasons. But if one goes for the right reasons, the ritual, the habit, the practice should increase the likelihood of one experiencing God. This is not, of course, because God is found in some buildings and on some days rather than others. We need special days and seasons because we—if we don't take special care to set aside times and put ourselves in places where God is the priority—can get so preoccupied and busy that we forget to look and listen for God.

Ritualism has given ritual a bad name. Perhaps we have forgotten how to enjoy it, how to profit by it. Perhaps we have never been instructed in how to profit by it, and so the ritual goes on without us. Perhaps we expect too much of it, that it will "work" too quickly, "deliver" too automatically, "function" in a foolproof way. But there, the real problem lies with our foolish expectations, doesn't it? I don't think we should give up on ritual. I don't think we should give up on any possible means of experiencing God.

3. Obedience/Self-Denial

Oddly, saints and sages throughout history will tell us that God is often found when we do things we don't want to do, or when we intentionally refrain from doing things we want to do. Consider these decidedly quotidian situations from daily life:

- A new coworker makes sexual advances toward you, and you are tempted to break your marriage vows, compromise your integrity, and put your whole family at risk through an affair.
- You are driving down the road, in a hurry because you are already late for an appointment, and you see a car broken down. Inside an old woman has her head leaning on the steering wheel, and it's clear she is crying.
- A relative has begun drinking too much, endangering his and others' safety when he drives, and sabotaging his marriage and career. Someone needs to speak sensitively but firmly to him about it, but everyone, including you, is too afraid. Or maybe the relative is you, and someone has just intervened and spoken to you, and you have a decision — to admit you have a problem and get help or to continue in your denial.
- You have made a choice you now regret — you have cheated on your spouse, or made a series of personal, long-distance phone calls from work, or failed to discipline your child because you craved his or her affection and approval too much. Immediately after feeling regret, another choice presents itself: either to admit that you have failed and done the wrong thing, or to make excuses.

Choices, Wrong and Right

In these moments, we make choices. Too often, we will all admit, we make the wrong choices. But people commonly agree that when they make the right choice (including the right choice of admitting our past wrong choices), a new experience of God often begins. There is a humility involved—realizing how vulnerable we are to doing wrong, to becoming bad people. There is also a kind of courage involved—to do the right thing even though our lust, our fear, our conceit, our greed, or our laziness is crying out against it. Jesus said something fascinating in this regard. "Anyone who chooses to do the will of God"—in other words, if a person wills to do what is right, even if it requires self-denial and personal sacrifice—"will find out whether my teaching comes from God." In another place, Jesus said that if a person loves and obeys him, he will disclose himself to that person, and God will "make our home with them." Spiritual enlightenment in this way seems to follow doing what is right. Doing what is right doesn't earn enlightenment (as in "goods paid for services rendered"), but it rather becomes a medium of enlightenment, just as doing wrong would reinforce us in our "disenlightenment," plunging us deeper into dark experiences of alienation, guilt, and shame rather than experiences of God, goodness, and love.

4. Worship/Art

I must put worship and art together, because in a real way, public worship is an experience of art, involving well-chosen words, music, architecture, perhaps sculpture, painting, film, drama, and dance as well. Sadly, too often public worship displays poor art, sloppy art, fake art—which may account for why many people find more distraction than help in their search for God at too many churches. But then again, often there is beauty, and sincerity, and best of all, in the best churches each attender is also a participant, helping make the music and say the words and use his or her gifts in the creation of something beautiful to celebrate the goodness of God.

I remember once being in Moedling, Austria, one of the places where Mozart lived. On a Sunday afternoon, my hosts and I were out for a walk, and we passed a beautiful church where a local orchestra and choir were holding a concert of Mozart's music. We didn't have tickets, and we were not dressed very formally, so we stood outside and listened to the whole church vibrate with the grandeur of Mozart's choral music. There were dozens of violinists and singers making music inside, but from the outside, the whole church and all it contained seemed to be a single instrument filling the town with glory. It became a single, composite work of art—a multisensory, multimedia event of sight, sound, feeling. I thought, "This is what the church should be—an instrument vibrant with beauty and grandeur and glory."

The house of worship you attend may use Mozart and Bach on pipe organ, hymns on a piano, contemporary music with electric guitars and drums, or sitar or bagpipes or dijeridoo or the instruments and music of some other culture. The architecture may be gothic, Victorian, or Shaker; you may worship in an old cathedral, a living room, or a school cafeteria. The liturgy (or format) may be ancient and formal or spontaneous and informal. But in just about every religious community, the experience of worship is intended at least to be an experience of beauty and glory. In that experience, you often can experience God.

Simple Prayers

Sometimes, the experience is very simple, and very subtle. I remember a time, many years ago, when I was going through a time of real spiritual struggle. I was full of doubts and wondered if God was real at all. My father asked me to attend a prayer meeting at his church. Most of the men there (there were only men) were three times my age. I had long hair and a beard and was probably dressed in blue jeans and an old T-shirt; they were clean-cut, white-haired or bald, in suits and ties. They spoke with "thee's and thou's," a practice I never appreciated, and the tone of their prayers was somber, almost grave. It was an experience almost guaranteed to alienate me. But I experienced God with them that evening. "I am so full of doubts and confusion about you," I remember praying silently, "but these men are so sure of you, and that is where I need to be tonight … around some people with a simple, proven faith who are surer of you than I am at this moment." The simple piety of their prayers became for me a work of art that carried me closer to God.

Other times, the experience of God in worship and prayer can be much more dramatic. A few weeks ago, for example, I was in Sydney, Australia, at a conference for mission leaders. Each day, a gifted woman named Jennifer sat at the piano and led us in songs of praise and worship. Jennifer works in inner-city Chicago, so many of her chosen songs were old Negro spirituals or more contemporary gospel songs. There were contemporary choruses too, and some old hymns. On the last day, as she led us and we sang and clapped and pondered the words of the songs, I felt overwhelmed with the presence of God. Tears streamed down my face for over an hour as we sang and praised God. There at that conference, I experienced something I can only call a spiritual reunion.

Imagine a person whom you love a great deal—a friend, a spouse, a parent—but someone from whom you are frequently separated, or perhaps someone who has died. If that person whom you miss so deeply suddenly, unexpectedly appeared in front of you, you would no doubt embrace with unbridled enthusiasm and speak fervent words of your love ... and perhaps cry too, for joy. Well, that is something of what I felt that day during a time of worship. God, whom I love but from whom I always feel some degree of distance simply because God is invisible (among other reasons), suddenly felt so near and real. It was as if God were standing right beside me, or even closer ... right inside me ... or even bigger, so I was right inside God ... and I felt embraced, contained, filled, saturated by God and God's love.

I suppose if I experienced this constantly, I would eventually grow used to it, and it would become a normal level of bliss or ecstasy for my daily living. In one way, that would be wonderful, but in another way, there is something equally wonderful about the comings and goings of these experiences. The times of absence make the times of "reunion" all the more precious; I can't help but feel I would take God more for granted if it were not for the feelings of absence at times — followed by these wonderful experiences of God's presence. (Similarly, if you lived in an art gallery every waking moment, wouldn't the paintings become mere furniture after a while, no more meaningful to you at any given moment than the calendar or whiteboard on your wall right now?)

Many of us experience God in worship more predictably and intensely than through any other means. As we sing and think about God's goodness, as we hear that goodness expressed through the well-chosen words of sermons and prayers and readings, and as it is celebrated through dance and drama and music and other art forms, we sense a Presence drawing near us. In the experience of that Presence, we feel reunited not only with God, but also with one another in a new way. That brings us to the next means of experiencing God.

5. Community

Those who seek for God generally agree that God is often found in other people, and more specifically, in the experience of loving and being loved by other people.

It hardly makes sense to try to describe this avenue of spiritual experience without telling some stories. Let me begin with an experience I shared with about 40,000 other pastors in 1996 in Atlanta, Georgia. A Christian organization sponsored the largest gathering of clergy in American history, and I must admit, I had mixed feelings about going—all the hype made me somewhat uncomfortable. The first two days of the event, I struggled with those mixed feelings. The messages seemed to me okay, but on the whole hardly worthy of the expense and effort and opportunity of an event like this. The times of worship and singing were extraordinary, of course, as you would expect, with 40,000 voices filling the indoor stadium. The hype came at various times, with some speakers eager to "make an impact" and trying a bit too hard for my taste.

But on the last day of the event, two themes emerged. The first theme had to do with reconciliation among denominations, and the second, with reconciliation among races. Representatives of North American native peoples, Hispanics, African Americans, Caucasians, and Asians all spoke of their desire to break down the walls, and experience true unity and brotherhood in God's love; all expressed true sorrow for their own versions of racism and isolation. What happened that day is hard to describe. There were tears, there were embraces, there were cheers, there was repentance. It felt like a baptism of love. I kept thinking of Jesus' words: "Where two or three come together in my name, there am I with them." I also thought of the beautiful Jewish poem in the Old Testament: "How good and pleasant it is when God's people live together in unity!... There the LORD bestows his blessing." I felt I was witnessing a beauty that probably would not be written up in the history books—but that probably had been seen few times in history. In some way that I am sure I am failing to convey, God was made real there, and in that experience of mass-community, we experienced God.

Friday Night Dinner

I should balance that story with something more intimate and personal. I can go back to an incident several years ago. Two of our good friends at church showed up unexpectedly at our door one evening. They sat on our couch in an uncomfortable silence. Finally the husband broke the silence, as the wife cried quietly. A trauma had hit their lives and their marriage, a very personal trauma, and they had been bearing it alone. "We can't keep this from our friends any longer. We feel like hypocrites covering this up. We need your help and support."

Over the next few days, they spoke to two other couples, and a week or so later, on a Friday night, the eight of us, plus all of our kids, had dinner together at our home. We talked some, we prayed some, but mostly we were just together. And we kept getting together, every Friday night, for about a year. No agenda, just to be together because two of our friends were suffering in a difficult time and needed to not suffer alone. There were no great epiphanies, but I think all of us look back on those Friday nights and think, "God was in that. We experienced God in those times. We experienced God in our friendship."

Sometimes — often, really — it's not as neat and sweet as that. I think of a situation in my church more recently, where somebody hurt somebody else's feelings, and told somebody else still, who took up the offense, and pretty soon a dozen people were mad at one another. I felt like I had taken my kids fishing and they had gotten their lines tangled in dozens of knots. In recent weeks, slowly people have been talking, seeing where they were wrong ... seeing where they believed the worst instead of the best ... hearing the other person's side of the story and seeing that they were doing the best they could, knowing what they knew ... and forgiving one another. And again, although it's messy, although nobody would choose to schedule experiences like this, it is often through these ugly and difficult times that forgiveness flows, love is deepened, and God seems present in a very real way — in community.

I think of many experiences where individuals or couples have come to me in my office, to discuss some personal problem or confess some sin or seek guidance in some way, and I had no idea what to say or do to help them. But as I listened and tried to simply be there with love in my heart, open to God like a window open to a breeze, there was this sense, by now a familiar sense, that we were not alone, and that the two or three of us had someone Else in our midst. I can't imagine how impoverished my experience of God would be if not for these experiences of community.

Your Response

1. I have experienced God in the following ways:

___Nature/Creation

___Ritual

___Obedience/Self-Denial

___Worship/Art

___Community

2. I am interested in further pursuing the following ways of experiencing God in the future:

___Nature/Creation

___Ritual

___Obedience/Self-Denial

___Worship/Art

___Community

3. Here is how I plan to pursue these ways of experiencing God:

Resources

Two books by Roman Catholic Henri Nouwen might be helpful: *Life of the Beloved: Spiritual Living in a Secular World* and *The Return of the Prodigal Son*. Greek Orthodox Archbishop Anthony Bloom has written a very helpful book, *Beginning to Pray*. Also check out Lauren Winner's *Mudhouse Sabbath*.

Prayer

God, thank you for the ways in which I feel I have experienced you or some aspect of you (grace, love, beauty, justice, purity) already in my life. It is not enough to say that I am open to experiencing more of you; I desire that experience ... I am hungry and thirsty for it. Like a child asking a parent for food and drink, protection and love, I ask you to reveal yourself to me, and to help me to truly experience you. I can not trump up or manufacture this, God. I can only ask you to help me.

How Else Might I Experience God?

This chapter, completing a survey of twelve ways people commonly experience God, looks at suffering, compassion, life-change, prayer, solitude, repentance, and joy.

Who Should Read This Chapter?

As in chapter 1, this chapter will be of special interest to people who want more than a conceptual approach to God and faith.

What Questions Does It Address?

Does spiritual experience strengthen faith, or is it the other way around? Suffering drives some people away from faith—how can it strengthen the faith of others? How does it feel to experience God through serving others compassionately? Why do people with life-controlling problems often turn to and experience God? Would an answered prayer offer complete proof for God's existence? Why is solitude helpful for spiritual seekers? What is the relationship between repentance and spiritual experience? Why is joy a common doorway into the experience of God?

God wishes to be seen, and he wishes to be sought, and he wishes to be expected, and he wishes to be trusted.

Julian of Norwich, *Julian of Norwich: Showings*

Now faith is the assurance of things hoped for, the conviction of things not seen.... whoever would draw near to God must believe that he exists and that he rewards those who seek him.

Hebrews 11:1, 6 RSV

"For I know the plans I have for you," declares the LORD, "plans to prosper you and not to harm you, plans to give you hope and a future. Then you will call on me and come and pray to me, and I will listen to you. You will seek me and find me when you seek me with all your heart. I will be found by you," declares the LORD.

Jeremiah 29:11–14

How Else Might I Experience God?

Which comes first, the spiritual experience or faith? Does faith create the spiritual experience, or does the experience create the faith? The answer to both questions is yes — spiritual experiences can create and strengthen faith, and yet they require some measure of preexisting faith to occur. So these categories of spiritual experience shouldn't be seen as formulaic prescriptions to achieve faith, as in, "engineer these experiences and faith will follow." You could as accurately try to guarantee that sex will engineer intimacy. Understand that the relationship between spiritual experiences and faith is more complex than a simple, linear cause and effect.

We have considered five ways whereby some people commonly experience God — through nature, ritual, self-denial, worship and art, and community. But other people would say that none of these ways have as of yet been very significant for them. They might point instead to times in which they felt comfort or sustenance in suffering, or times when they were able to bring comfort to others. Or they might recall turnaround experiences in their lives, or perhaps some inexplicable "coincidence" that seemed to be a divine intervention. Or they might share stories of times when they were in solitude but didn't feel alone, or when they sensed mercy and forgiveness in the midst of regret after wrongdoing, or when a peak experience of joy somehow convinced them that God was real. To those avenues of experiencing God we now turn.

6. Suffering

In suffering, people often feel abandoned by God. They cry and pray for relief, and relief doesn't come, and the questions just echo ... why? why now? why me? why him or her? For many people, it is suffering that drives them to atheism or agnosticism.

Yet to be fair, there are many others who say the opposite. I think of an older woman who told me this story. She had a heart disease and pneumonia, and she was in the hospital. One night she was having great difficulty breathing, and the thought hit her for the first time: *I may die before daybreak tomorrow.* At first, she felt a panic, which only made her more desperate for breath and threatened to throw her into a frenzy that could perhaps kill her. "I've got to calm down," she told herself. "What can I do?" And then the thought came to her, "I'll pray." And as she prayed, she told me a peace came over her—a peace she had never experienced before. The fear of dying left her. She eventually drifted off to sleep, and each time she awoke, she asked herself, "Is the peace still there?" And each time, it was. "Brian," she told me, "I've always heard people tell stories like this, but I never experienced anything like it myself. But since that night, I've known that God is real—real in a way I never imagined I could know."

One of the benefits of finding a faith community (as we will consider more deeply in a later chapter) is that you surround yourself with people who have stories like this to tell. And one of the benefits of continuing to search for God in the midst of suffering (rather than assuming God has abandoned you) is that eventually you will have some stories of your own.

Opposite Responses

As I said, though, sometimes suffering drives people from faith. For many years, my friend Larry Culp edited a newsletter called *Network*. It linked the community of adults living with cystic fibrosis (CF), of which Larry was a member. He devoted one issue (April 1997) to religion and CF, and the essays it contained conveyed powerfully the variety of responses to this horrible disease. Consider this collage of quotes from that issue:

> I had always believed in God and then my health began to seriously deteriorate.... When I finally had to receive a liver transplant, I had had enough and was through with God.... I was very ill and though I prayed every day to get better, I only got worse.... I was appalled and seriously [ticked off] at God.... Everyone always says that I should thank God that I am alive, and part of me wants to. But the other part of me thanks myself, and the people who love me, for wanting to fight to get better.
>
> *Jennifer, 21*

> Today I am not bitter, but at peace with having CF. Through my suffering, I've been able to grow and contemplate life in ways many people my age have not.... My mind and eyes have been opened to God's glory through my struggles with CF. I have been blessed.
>
> *Carolyn, 23*

I had cystic fibrosis and I was gonna have to learn to deal with it. Maybe that's when I started to think in terms of the physical world, for lack of a better term, as being the only world that I would live in.... I majored in biology.... I took these teachings as my new "religion," having learned to have faith in the scientific method. The "miracle" of life, which some say is God's gift, now seemed nothing more to me than a complicated set of chemical reactions. Very complex, surely ... but requiring the Hand of God? I saw no such need for such hocus-pocus.... I do not feel the need for a grand master plan put forth by some omnipotent being, nor do I feel that there is such a being watching over us every day, acknowledging us and our prayers. I don't believe any more.

Kenneth, 39

... The door slammed shut and I was in the dark again. I don't have the key anymore ... and I will never trust in God again. I will never pray again either because I prayed ... every day and my prayers were never answered.... I try and take each day as they come, along with the pain and loneliness, but I know that only time can heal that, and not God.

Jennifer, 22

As I read these powerful and poignant stories for the first time, I wondered how Larry himself was dealing with his illness and integrating it with his faith. Editing all these intensely personal essays must have only intensified his own struggles, I thought. Then I came upon his own piece near the end of the newsletter:

> I have been through most of these dark, emotional places, places familiar to many who have CF. Even today, it's easy to regress.... My faith teaches me to look in and to look out. To look in at what's wrong with me, and to look out to serve others. This is against my typical proclivity to look out at what's wrong with others, and look in to serve myself.... I don't know why God allows horrible things to happen in this world.... In my own small way, I can do my part to make sure I am not part of the world's problems, but part of the solution.... I try not to allow CF to color my view of God, but try to allow God to color my view of CF.... I don't know where I'd be without God in my life.
>
> *Larry, 37*

The same variety of responses to life, paradoxically, is present among those who are healthy, rich, free, privileged, advantaged. It's odd. Like Larry, there is a lot I have no idea how to explain. And like Larry, I make no editorial comment at all on those whose suffering has driven them from faith, or faith from them. All I can do is hope that I can be of some help or comfort or encouragement, as Larry was while he was still with us.

7. Compassion

The suffering of others can indeed pose even greater challenges to faith than our own suffering. But when we leverage ourselves into the situation in the right way, even the suffering of others can open for us experiences of God, especially as we are taken up into being part of the solution to their suffering. In our anger or frustration, we might pray, "God, why do you allow this? Why don't you do something?" And at that moment, God has every reason to say something like this to us: "I have done something: I have placed you in the situation with a compassionate heart and the ability to help. Now you can become an expression of my concern." Obviously, few of us ever hear these kinds of messages directly from God, and most often, we only realize the significance of our involvement in retrospect.

Where Was God?

A friend of mine has been learning about history's atrocities — Hitler, Pol Pot, the Plague, the Rwandan genocide, colonialism, and so forth. His conclusion: If God exists, God must be dispassionate, incapable of feeling any compassion, uncaring, apathetic. Someday I want to explore this thought with him: Might my friend's own compassion, his outrage, his deep feeling itself be a reflection of the care of God? In other words, if God were dispassionate, how could God create beings with compassion? Perhaps at least a partial answer to the question, "Where was God during the Holocaust?" is this: God was and is in every person feeling compassion and outrage. If no one felt any compassion or any outrage, then we would have reason to believe in a dispassionate God. And perhaps the answer goes even further: God was in those being tortured, mistreated, killed — suffering and dying with them. Perhaps this will help my friend. Probably not. Probably there is no answer to make this problem more tolerable; probably our best response is not to try to devise an intellectual system that accounts for suffering, but rather to feel the outrage and compassion and be driven by them to action.

Sometimes we see God in the caring faces of those who care for the suffering. Sometimes we see God in the agonized faces of those who suffer themselves. Jesus alluded to this kind of experience when he told the parable about the naked and homeless, the destitute, the imprisoned criminals, the shut-ins with chronic diseases who had been visited by his followers. To those who had shown compassion in various ways to their needy neighbors, God says, "Whatever you did for one of the least of these brothers and sisters of mine, you did for me." In other words, we can experience God as we show compassion, and we can also experience God in the person who receives our compassion.

A Lone Shoe on a Sheet of Ice

I remember one morning my wife and I were driving in our neighborhood. It was a cold winter morning, and on a side street something unusual caught my eye as I drove past. It was a single shoe on a patch of ice in the middle of the road. I took a second glance and saw on one corner a young boy near tears, and on the other corner, an old man, legs splayed on the sidewalk, lying there in bare feet! We stopped, turned around, and got out of our car. It was a pathetic sight in this typical suburban neighborhood. The gentleman, African, unable to speak English, was reaching out to us with both hands, terror in his eyes, speaking a mile a minute. On the other corner, the boy, his grandson as it turned out, was screaming, "Please help us. Please help us."

The boy explained: "This is my grandfather. He is from Ethiopia. He just arrived yesterday. He has never been in the cold before. He wanted to walk me to school and then he fell on the ice. He is not used to walking in shoes, and he never before saw ice. His shoes fell off when he fell and he says he can't walk, and I think I am already late for school...." We got the boy in the front seat and gingerly helped the old man into the backseat. It was clear his leg was broken badly. He was in a lot of pain.

We took the boy to school and then took the man to his son's home. His daughter-in-law, an immigrant whose English was quite good, came out, and the three of us got him inside. We made sure she knew how to get him to a hospital, and as we left, the man — his face full of a mixture of pain and relief — wouldn't stop talking to us, obviously thanking us although we couldn't understand his words. The whole episode took less than fifteen minutes, but it brought with it an experience of God that lingered for days — and that is with me now as I retell it.

It hits me on multiple levels. On one level, I think, "Here was a man who was in real need. people kept driving by, and he was cold and afraid, and it seemed that no one cared. But God cared about him, and God made sure Grace and I came along, noticed him, and helped him. What a privilege to be instruments of God's love, agents of God's compassion!" On another level, I think, "God, you were in that old man in need. When I came to him, I found you there. In showing love for that man, in simply being his neighbor, I was given the privilege of finding you in a new way, in a new place ... and even more, I was given the honor of in some small way showing love for you."

8. Life-Change

Have you ever attended an Alcoholics Anonymous (AA) meeting, or any similar meeting (NA, CDA, and so on)? You will better understand this means of experiencing God powerfully if you attend a few meetings with a friend in recovery. At nearly every meeting you will hear a true story from someone whose life had gone out of control due to some form of addiction. This person realized that he was completely powerless over his addiction, and eventually reached "bottom," a point where he despaired of his own ability to change his own unmanageable life through his own willpower. At that bottom point, he reached out to God — a Higher Power outside of himself of whom he admittedly had little understanding — and in the days, weeks, and months that followed, he found that this outside power was restoring him to sanity. Over time, he learned more about this power. For example, he learned that God was morally good and that part of God's healing process involved not only release from addiction, but release from moral anarchy; the person will tell you about how he engaged in a searching moral inventory, identifying his wrongs and seeking, wherever possible, to make amends to those he had hurt.

He also learned that this Higher Power cared about others, and so he began to dedicate himself to carrying the message of a caring, restoring God to others in similar pain. In addition, he learned that he would very easily relapse unless he sought to maintain constant conscious contact with God through prayer and meditation, and to practice moral discipline in all of his daily affairs.

Story after story you will hear, and even though the room might be filled with cigarette smoke, and four-letter words will likely be as common as "amens" and "hallelujahs" are at church, you will sense the presence of God. At least I know I have.

The Only Idiots

I will never forget my first AA meeting. Before entering ministry, I was a college English teacher. I taught at a small college in Washington, DC, for a while, and one day I arrived at the school only to find the lights off and no one there. My first thought was, "Is this the day when the clocks are changed? Am I here an hour early?" But it wasn't the last week of October, so I was still mystified. I walked down to the office, and I knew something was strange when I saw the coordinator's door open ... and one of my colleagues (not the coordinator) seated in her chair with his feet on her desk. He motioned for me to come in and laughed: "So you and I are the only idiots who didn't know that classes were canceled today." We discussed the fact that everyone else had, apparently, been notified that there would be no classes that day due to some major renovations in the building. I got ready to go home. Then Bill said, "Hey Brian, can I ask you a personal question?"

Bill, I should tell you, had a PhD in philosophy and was a very bright, very cynical atheist who had been ribbing me somewhat good-naturedly ever since he found out I was a committed Christian. So I wasn't surprised when he asked, "What's a nice guy like you doing in a disgusting religion like Christianity?" I laughed and said, "What kind of question is that to hit me with at eight o'clock on a Monday morning?" Then this cynical guy seemed to get tears in his eyes.

"Brian," he said, "can we talk for a minute?" I nodded, and then there was a pause, then this: "You know me. You know I have a real problem with this God thing. Well—and you're the first person I've told this to—two weeks ago I admitted that I have an alcohol problem, and I've been sober for two weeks—the longest period of sobriety I've had since I was about thirteen. When I got here about a half hour ago, I was terrified. I thought—oh no, I have a whole day on my hands with nothing to do — and I felt the urge to go out and drink. AA keeps telling me about this Higher Power bit, but I don't buy it yet. But then I prayed anyway, and right after that, you walk in the door. Kind of spooky, huh?"

We went out to breakfast, and he told me his story, and we hung out together until the day's first AA meeting in the area, which I attended with him. Both of us felt we had experienced God in a real way, in the process of Bill's life-change.

9. Prayer/Intervention

Bill's answered prayer was definitely an experience of God for him — even though he wasn't sure whether he even believed in God or prayer yet! And I can tell you so many stories from my own life where I have felt the direct intervention of God — plus, as a pastor, I am in contact with hundreds of people each with dozens of stories of their own. Put together, those stories are pretty compelling evidence for God's existence and involvement in our lives. I have to admit, though, that the stories have a problematic edge to them.

Take, for example, the story of my friend Tim, who lives in Tasmania, Australia. Once, he and his wife were traveling from Melbourne to Sydney for a conference. They had left their children with friends in Melbourne and were traveling in a friend's car. It's a long drive, so they left at about 5:00 a.m., and most if not all of the passengers were soon asleep. At about 7:00 a.m., the driver fell asleep at the wheel, and the car flew off the road at a high speed and flipped end over end down a steep hill. It landed — almost as if placed there by a huge hand — upside down in a gully, the gully just being deep enough so that the cab of the car was not crushed. Other drivers saw the accident and jumped out, assuming the worst because they couldn't see the cab-sized gully beneath the car below them. Nobody even tried to come down to the wreck, because it looked obvious that no one could survive such a crash. The car appeared flattened to them.

Meanwhile, the passengers were all hanging upside down in their seat belts, and one by one, they managed to unlatch themselves, fall to the ceiling, and crawl out the broken windows. Imagine everyone's surprise when every one of them, driver included, emerged with no broken bones, no serious injuries, just bruises and scratches.

A Dream and a Prayer

Three weeks later, Tim and his wife were back in Tasmania and they got a letter from a good friend, a woman living in India. She wrote because three weeks earlier she had had a terrible dream of her friends being in an accident. The dream was so alarming that it awoke her from a sound sleep at 4:00 a.m., and she felt compelled to get out of bed, get on her knees, and pray for her friends' safety. The next morning, she thought there must not have been anything to the dream because the car in her dream was bright red (and she knew their car wasn't red) and because the children weren't present (and this couple was seldom separated from their kids). She was just writing to make sure they were okay.

Imagine Tim's surprise when he realized, yes, the car they had been in was bright red, and that, accounting for the time difference, their friend had awakened at exactly the same time as their accident. A remarkable story (and, I assure you, a true one from a credible person, not some superstitious kook who likes to tell exaggerated or fabricated tales). But, of course, the story raises a lot of questions. What about all the accidents where cars don't conveniently find lifesaving gullies to land in? Did God care less for those people? And wouldn't have God saved these people if no one had prayed? Why give this woman this dream? What role did her prayer have in the whole thing?

I tell the story — and include the problematic edges — because I think that prayer, whether answered or unanswered, isn't as simple a subject as many of us preachers make it appear to be. Prayer certainly doesn't work like a scientific experiment that can be repeatedly validated under controlled conditions. But having said that, if you are ever on the receiving end of one of these miraculous "coincidences," you have this strong feeling that, problematic issues notwithstanding, you have experienced God. Many of you know what I mean.

10. Solitude

It's funny about solitude — for introverted people, solitude feels like a vacation, but for the more extroverted, it feels like a punishment, as in solitary confinement. But extroverts and introverts alike will agree that there is something to be said for getting away from other people for extended periods of time — half a day, a day, a weekend, a week, even more — to have a time where the only companionship available for your soul is the presence of God.

One value of solitude is seen in the beautiful parable about the lost (or prodigal) son, told by Jesus and recorded in Luke 15. A runaway boy squanders his wealth on wine, women, and parties. When he has spent all his money, not surprisingly he finds he has also lost his popularity. Destitute, he gets a job feeding pigs (a deplorable job for a good Jewish boy). And nobody will talk to him. It is in that forced solitude, the story goes, that the boy "comes to himself." And this coming to oneself then opens him to the possibility of coming home to his father and his true home.

Recollecting My Ghost Images

Solitude has a similar value for me. In my busyness, in my many roles, in the context of many demands and projects and goals, it is easy to lose touch with myself. And when I am out of touch with myself, it's hard — perhaps impossible — to get in touch with God. Why? Because there is no solid "me" to bring into contact with God. I am a composite of ghost images, like an out-of-focus TV. But in solitude, I recollect all of these out-of-sync selves and we are reconstituted into a more solid me ... and that reconstituted me is the person who can "come home" to God.

Again, I don't want to raise unrealistic hopes. There are times when I try to draw away for solitude, and rather than having a great experience of God, my mind is filled with more confusion and turmoil, or I am plagued by worry or lust (hardly a great spiritual experience) or a feeling of spiritual dullness in which God's absence rather than presence feels accentuated.

The Spiritual Side of Fishing

It seems strangely fitting to me, in this regard, that many of the first followers of Jesus were fishermen. I am an avid fisherman myself, and this whole search for God has many similarities to fishing. In my office hangs a framed picture given me a few years back by my staff members (who know how I spend my days off), which contains this quote in beautiful calligraphy:

"The charm of fishing is that it is the pursuit of what is elusive but attainable—a perpetual series of occasions for hope." And I suppose that is how it is with solitude and the other means of experiencing God we are considering. One can put oneself in the right place in the right frame of mind, and then one must wait, but not passively—rather, actively, as a fisherman waits with his line in the water, or as a farmer waits after he has planted his crops—leaving the outcome to God. That's where faith comes in ... believing that there will be a tug on the line or that the fields will come to life and in time bear a harvest.

11. Repentance/Grace

Repentance is an essential part of the coming to oneself that is in turn an essential part of solitude. And it is in the context of repentance that many people find their initial experience of God. Repentance literally means to give something a second thought, to think again, to see life and oneself in a new light, to turn a corner, to "do a 180." Repentance is like exercise or dieting in some ways: just about everybody needs it, but it is amazingly easy to avoid.

If someone else comes to you telling you that you need to repent, there is a good chance you will react defensively: "Who are you to judge me? You have plenty of faults of your own. I am not so bad. Why focus on my few faults and ignore the many good things about me? There are plenty of worse people than me for you to pick on!"

But there are times in life when nobody has to tell us—we are telling ourselves: "I haven't got this right. I don't like what I am becoming. There's something wrong in the way I am living. And it's not just outward behaviors either; those outward behaviors are fueled by something inside me ... and that's where the problem is. Something deep within me is broken, sick; it needs to be fixed, healed." We might have specific data to deal with, telling us we are broken inside — another broken relationship, another broken marriage, another broken promise, another broken dream. Or we might just have this nagging feeling of guilt, a sense that we have taken the easy way, the path of least resistance ... that we have gone with the flow and in some way lost our souls in the process.

Humble Beginnings

That kind of reflection — where we see ourselves and think again about what direction we want to take in the future, sure that it is a very different direction than we have taken so far — often puts us in a frame of heart and mind where we experience God. Why is this? Here's my guess: At those moments where we freely admit our wrongs, we are as close as we ever get to being truly humble. At those moments there is a response that comes from God, a personal response so natural and strong that it can't be stopped, like a hand instantly reaching out to a companion who falls, or like a mother's instinctive turn when she hears her child's cry. The words the theologians use for this pure, spontaneous response is "grace" — amazing grace.

Grace is what a father feels (and a son receives) when he catches his son doing something wrong, and the boy (instead of defending himself or blaming his little brother or making an excuse or telling a pathetic lie to cover it up) bursts into tears and says, "I am sorry." Punishment seems unnecessary; a stern word even seems out of place. The father takes the boy in his arms and simply says, "It's okay. I love you."

When we experience the grace of God in this way, it can be one of life's most significant events.

12. Joy

Sometimes the search for God is activated by peak experiences of joy. My contemporaries might remember a gravely-voiced musician from the 60s named Barry McGuire, best known for his hit "Eve of Destruction" and his work with The New Christy Minstrels. One summer "back in the day," I played backup guitar for another musician (Scott Wesley Brown), and I was fortunate enough to be Barry's trailer-mate at a large outdoor music festival. I will never forget a story Barry used to tell in his concerts ...

One of his nonmusical jobs was working on a fishing boat out of a little town called San Pedro, California. One day, after a long day of fishing, a school of dolphins swam up alongside the boat. Barry leaned over and admired their beauty through the clear Pacific water as they swam just beneath the surface, keeping pace with the boat. One dolphin in particular seemed to look up at him. Barry felt this crazy impulse, this wild urge to somehow make contact with the animal. But how? Almost without thinking, he grabbed a towel from the deck, tied a knot in the end, and leaned over the edge of the boat. The next time the dolphin surfaced, Barry swung the towel and whacked the dolphin playfully. To his surprise, the dolphin seemed to like the game, and for the next several minutes, Barry was laughing and "yahooing" and whacking dolphins, as more and more surfaced and seemed to playfully imply, "Hit me! Me too!" The play lasted for some time, and then the school moved away from the boat.

A Gift

In the silent moments that followed, as the exhilaration calmed to a peaceful contentment, Barry says he felt something ... a sense that this experience was a gift, a gift from his creator ... and he felt in the experience of joy a certain call, a homeward call, a call toward God. The great scholar and writer C. S. Lewis described similar experiences in his autobiography, *Surprised by Joy*. In each pure experience of joy was a hint of something more, a call to find an even greater joy, a joy of the spirit, a joy of being connected to God. My friend Michael Kelly Blanchard expresses it well in one of his songs, called, "Thanks Be to God." As life's pleasures and joys come our way, the sense that there is someone to thank is, in a real way, an experience of God. These experiences really are a gift, and if a gift, then there must be a giver.

Who do you thank at the gate of the dawn as the hounds
of the night back away?
Who do you thank for the morning's new song, sung by
birds as they play?
Who do you thank for the sermon of sun
Preaching the hope of a new day begun,
Testifying that love's light has won?
Who do you thank for this kingdom come?

... Who do you thank for this mural of life,
the savor of senses sharp as a knife,
the privilege of poignant, the honor of right?
Who do you thank for delight?...

Who do you thank for the treasure of home, wrapped in
the real of routine,

The blessing of knowing your own flesh and bone, and
    watching them wake from your dream?
Who do you thank for the structure of souls,
tied to each other from infant to old,
beauty so human, so holy to hold?
Who do you thank for such gold?

"Mercy in the Maze"

After completing his interviews and research for a fascinating book on prayer, radio host Larry King (a self-described agnostic who doesn't — not yet, anyway — "sign my name to God's starting roster") was surprised to feel the same nudge toward gratitude that Blanchard so beautifully celebrated in his song. King recalls a conversation with the rabbi who had been his advisor in the writing project:

"I can't give up on you, Larry, I am a rabbi.... I can't make you pray, Larry. Nobody can do that. The answer's right in front of you. It's right inside you. But it's something you have to want to find. I can only point the way. In the end, you must take the final steps of the journey alone."

... I watched his black yarmulke disappear into the morning crowd. When I could see him no longer, I headed in the opposite direction, toward Central Park South. As I crossed the street it occurred to me that I didn't have to be anywhere for another hour, so I decided to meander.... Today I made a point of looking at the city with fresh eyes, listening to the sounds of the street and smelling the fresh spring air. At Columbus Circle, waiting to cross into Central Park, I remember saying quietly, "Thank you." I suppose it was for the blessings of being alive, finally having a fabulous wife, feeling wonderful, being surrounded by a vibrant, vital city—all of that. I can't honestly say to whom that "thank you" was directed, but I know I wasn't talking to myself. (Larry King, *Powerful Prayers*, 1998)

A small step perhaps, but a step of faith nonetheless.

This List Is Incomplete

We have considered a number of means by which we might experience God. This is not, of course, an exhaustive list. The whole point is that there is not just one or just two or even just twelve ways in which God might speak to us, make contact with us, become experience-able by us. Perhaps you have heard the story about Saint Augustine, before he was anything close to being a saint. He was a womanizer, a partier, with little concern for God or morality. One day, outside his window some children were playing. They had a little chant they said as part of their games: "Take and read, take and read." It seemed to Augustine that God was speaking to him through those children ... to take up a copy of the Bible and read it. He did, and he experienced God. Which category in our list would that experience fit under?

God seems to be amazingly creative in finding ways to connect with us. For me, a few words of a conversation sometimes have struck me with the force of revelation, or a scene in a movie seemed to be "meant" for me at that time, or the line of a song, or even the music itself, seemed to be inspired for me in a particular life situation. And so at unexpected moments, these serendipitous experiences of God come, as C. S. Lewis said, by surprise.

Perhaps, if we were a little more awake, a little more open, if we looked up from our trivial pursuits a little more often, we would find that the experience of God is far more common than we had realized. One of C. S. Lewis's mentors, George MacDonald, believed that the "smallest chink" of openness could make a difference.

A Wise Rabbi

I remember hearing the story of an old Jewish rabbi who said something similar when approached by a young agnostic. "I can't see God anywhere," the young man explained. "Can you help me?" "I don't think so," the old rabbi answered, "because I can't identify with your problem. You see, I can't not see God." And of course, in this way, simply by sharing his experience, the old rabbi did help the young man. Perhaps when we are old, and when we are farther along on our search, and when our eyes are better trained, we will be like the old rabbi. And perhaps we will be able to remember what it was like before we had experienced God, so that we can understand those who are as we used to be.

So, how might God be experienced? We have considered many ways. Which ways have you explored? If all of them are new to you, which ones should be your starting points?

Your Response

1. I have experienced God in the following ways:

   ___Suffering
   ___Compassion
   ___Life-change

___Prayer/Intervention

___Solitude

___Repentance/Grace

___Joy

2. I am interested in further pursuing the following ways of experiencing God in the future:

___Suffering

___Compassion

___Life-change

___Prayer/Intervention

___Solitude

___Repentance/Grace

___Joy

3. Here is how I plan to pursue these ways of experiencing God:

Resources

Regarding the profound subject of experiencing God in pain and suffering, five writers stand out. C. S. Lewis's *The Problem of Pain* has helped thousands, including me. Peter Kreeft's *Making Sense Out of Suffering* builds on Lewis's more philosophical work, and to a degree personalizes it. Philip Yancey's *Where Is God When It Hurts?* and *Disappointment with God* are also excellent. Some have criticized Rabbi Harold Kushner's *When Bad Things Happen to Good people* for theological imprecision, but on a popular level it has also helped thousands. And Joni Eareckson Tada's books, beginning with her autobiography *Joni*, speak from the vantage point of a woman who has suffered the pains and deprivations of being a quadriplegic. You also might want to find Amy Grant's song, "Somewhere Down the Road" too, on *Behind the Eyes* (A&M Records, 1997); in 5 minutes and 9 seconds, it says a lot and says it well.

Those with a background or interest in psychology and counseling might benefit from the writings of M. Scott Peck (such as *The Road Less Traveled*) and Paul Tournier. Tournier's integration of hard science (he was a medical doctor before becoming a counselor), social science (psychology and psychiatry), and spirituality is rich and has helped me greatly. Some of his books are hard to find, but others have been reissued; look especially for *The Adventure of Living*.

As for artistic explorations of the experience of God, the films *The Color Purple* and *Chariots of Fire* depict dramatic and poignant experiences, as do the wonderful ramblings of Garrison Keillor (in his enchanting Lake Wobegon books and tapes). As a preacher, I would have to say that Keillor's stories are better at simply conveying grace than 90 percent (maybe even 100) of the sermons I have preached.

Why not listen to Bach or Mozart, or Handel's *Messiah*—not just as a student of their music, but as a seeker for God? A trip to the art gallery in this spirit could also be very productive. I wish you could catch the spiritual zest of my friend Bob Jackson's paintings, which flow from a faith-enriched vision of life (www.robertcjackson.com). Or perhaps there are cathedrals, chapels, or other structures designed for people of faith nearby for you to visit, to see how the art of architects can help you in your spiritual quest.

Prayer

God, could it be true that you surround me like the sea, and that even a small chink in the walls of my heart would allow you to rush in? Could it ever be true that you would be more real to me? This is my hope and my request. Maybe a greater experience of you will come through your presence in my own suffering or through my attempt to help someone else who is suffering. Maybe it will come through some impossible coincidence or intervention I experience in my life—a need for help, for change, for companionship, or for forgiveness. Maybe it will be through a moment of joy, when I will feel grateful and will finally know whom to thank.

I would like to tell you, God, what I currently understand you to be like. (Continue on your own, using the adjectives that you believe are descriptive to God. You can simply say, "I believe you are ...") *I am sure all of my understandings are partial; I ask you to deepen my understanding of you. If any of my understandings are wrong or misguided, please guide me and redirect my thinking. I want to have an accurate understanding of you, and a closer and closer relationship with you.*

Can I Experience God through Doubt?

This chapter looks at times when faith is stretched or shaken, and suggests that even doubt can be a channel for more deeply relating to God.

Who Should Read This Chapter?

This chapter will be especially helpful to people whose faith is being undermined because of emotional or physical pain, or who simply don't "feel" close to God.

What Questions Does It Address?

What is the difference between doubting "against" and "with" God? Why does anger at God actually reveal a level of faith and commitment to God?

I stretch lame hands of faith, and grope,
    And gather dust and chaff, and call
    To what I feel is Lord of all,
And faintly trust the larger hope....

Canto 55

There lives more faith in honest doubt,
Believe me, than in half the creeds....

Canto 96

That which we dare invoke to bless;
    Our dearest faith; our ghastliest doubt;
    He, They, One, All; within, without;
The Power in darkness whom we guess....
No, like a child in doubt and fear;
    But that blind clamor made me wise;
    Then was I as a child that cries,
But, crying, knows his father near;
And what I am beheld again
    What is, and no man understands;
    And out of darkness came the hands
That reach through nature, molding men.

Canto 124

Alfred, Lord Tennyson, "In Memoriam"

3

Can I **Experience God** through **Doubt?**

We have been talking about many "positive" ways of experiencing God, but there is another side to the story—a side we may be more familiar with than we wish. The great mystics through history tell us of "dark nights of the soul," of the "absence of God," of spiritual dryness and depression, of times of anger with God, of the experience of spiritual abandonment—where God feels distant, silent, nonexistent to the very person who once felt so near, so secure, so sure in his relationship with God. Sometimes it is surprising to me that these great spiritual leaders have these experiences. I don't know whether to feel encouraged (that I have these experiences in common with them) or depressed (that there is, apparently, no escaping them). What is even more surprising to me, and wholly more encouraging, is this: These spiritual pioneers tell us that in the end, these "negative" spiritual experiences have drawn them closer to God and strengthened their faith.

I used to feel very worried—even guilty—about the episodes of doubt or spiritual depression that came my way. But gradually I am starting to realize what the great mystics of the past knew: God can be experienced through doubt and other spiritual "diseases." So, I am learning more and more to doubt with God, instead of against God. Let me explain this important distinction by telling a story.

Doubting with God

Paul was one of my best friends growing up. We were adventurous boys and rowdy teenagers together — and we both became committed followers of God during the same time period too. We got married the same weekend and stood in one another's weddings (his wedding was on Saturday, mine on Sunday, which delayed his honeymoon — so his was the greater sacrifice by far!). We had kids around the same times, and both of us had children with some serious health problems: a few years before my third child was diagnosed with cancer, Paul's oldest child needed open heart surgery.

I remember visiting Paul and Josh in the ICU after surgery. Paul was bent over the bed, his face just a few inches from Josh's face. Josh was hooked up to all kinds of technology via tubes and wires. Josh was crying, groaning, screaming with a hoarse voice — his chest hurt so bad. And as I came closer, I could see what else Josh was doing: he was pounding on his father's chest. His fists were pounding out a message his little mind couldn't yet articulate: "You're my father! You're supposed to protect me! You're not protecting me! This is your fault! I am in pain! I am angry at you! I hate you! I think you must hate me to put me in this hospital and subject me to this pain! You're a bad father! I must punish you! I don't trust you anymore! I don't love you anymore!"

Empathy for God

I can only imagine what Paul must have felt. Driving home, I felt empathy for Paul, an empathy that would be intensified a few years later as I had to hold down my crying, writhing son while he got spinal taps and bone marrow tests as part of cancer treatment. That day, driving home, I not only felt empathy for Paul, I also felt empathy for God. I saw how my doubts are often much like Josh's little fists — trying to express my pain, my rage, my terror, at being in situations I don't want to be in, difficulties I can't understand, predicaments I can't solve. And there God is, loving me so much that he draws even closer so I can hit him all the harder … because he understands that's what I need to do.

So I am learning to see not just doubt, but also faith in Josh's fists. After all, he doesn't lash out at the nurses. He doesn't cry to the doctors. He doesn't punch the nurse's aids. He doesn't expect anything of them. It's his very connection to his father that makes him express his furious doubts to him. It's his very love for his father that forces him to say, through his fists, "I hate you." And, I am learning, it is my faith in God that forces me to sometimes doubt him.

They say that the opposite of love isn't hate; it is rather indifference. And I have to think that the same is true of faith. Doubt isn't a spiritual danger sign nearly as much as indifference would be.

Doubting My Faith versus Doubting God

There is something else I have learned. Doubting my faith isn't the same as doubting God. My faith is my own creation — a worldview, a paradigm, a map for life, a set of guiding principles — that I am assembling and reassembling from what I read, who I know and respect, what I experience, and so forth. My faith isn't perfect, and it isn't static. It is guaranteed by my finitude to be incomplete, inaccurate in many places, out of proportion, in need of continuing midcourse corrections. Therefore, it deserves to be doubted at times — doubted so it can be corrected.

If I didn't doubt my faith, I would protect it, not correct it; defend it, not amend it.

So I am learning that when I doubt my faith, I don't have to doubt God. In fact, doubting my faith can be an opportunity for increased faith in God. A proverb in the Old Testament says as much: "Trust in the LORD with all your heart and lean not on your own understanding; in all your ways submit to him, and he will make your paths straight." There is a difference — subtle but very significant — between having faith in my faith (i.e., faith in my intellectual concepts about God — another way of saying "leaning on my own understanding") and having faith in God. There is a corresponding difference between doubting my faith and doubting God.

When I doubt my faith, when I can't lean on it because I am not sure it will hold my full weight, then I can paradoxically more fully lean on God with my whole heart. At those times, my prayers sound like this: "God, I don't understand anything very clearly right now, including you. My certainty and confidence levels are low. But I still believe you are good — better than my best flawed understanding of you. So I am reaching out to you, calling out to you, asking you for your help, in the middle of my doubts. I feel as if I am walking in the dark, and I don't want to stumble or wander from the good path. Guide me in the path, Lord. Direct me."

Held in a Grasp Stronger Than Our Own

Those kinds of prayers don't feel very full of faith. They feel desperate, weak, pitiful. But I wonder, from God's perspective, if they aren't the expressions of the greatest faith of all ... like a person hanging over a cliff, holding on to a saving hand, who reaches a point of saying, "I can't hold on anymore. I am trusting you to hold me. It's your grip on me, not my grip on you, that will rescue me. It's all up to you." Can you see the faith in those words? You might say, "It's an unrealistic situation, though. I've never been hanging from a cliff." But, of course, you have. Part of being human, it seems, is the awareness that we are hanging over a precipice, susceptible to the horrible gravity of despair or greed, lust or laziness, ambition or addiction, hedonism or nihilism. (For a vivid description of this experience of hanging in space, see Tolstoy's dream in the final pages of his *Confession*.) In our times of strength and confidence, we say, "I can save myself." There's no faith in that, really. It's only when we feel utterly incapable of saving ourselves that faith becomes relevant. (Of course, "relevant" is a gross understatement at those times.) We hate those times of weakness, but I can see why life would be engineered to bring us to them; without them, we might never learn what faith is at all. Someone has said that you never know if your faith is real until it is all you have left.

Old Friend in a New Way

Several years ago, I had a falling out with a very good friend and coworker in the church. We represented two different forces in the church, and those forces were in tension, so our friendship nearly snapped under the strain. We were still committed to one another, because in principle, as Christians, we believe in reconciliation. But our relationship didn't seem much like a friendship anymore, and it was more a source of discomfort to both of us than of pleasure.

A few days ago, we met for breakfast. Even though we have been somewhat awkward with each other, we have tried to keep getting together—not every week, as we had done years ago, but every few months, just out of commitment to our belief in reconciliation, out of stubborn refusal to let go and call the relationship over forever. Recently, we had breakfast—and both of us sensed that something had shifted. Somehow, we felt that we had both gotten beyond our differences, and this time, instead of feeling it was hard work to keep the conversation going, laughter flowed, and vulnerability flowed, and we found ourselves asking for one another's advice and prayers and help. We dropped our empty coffee cups and bagel crumbs in the trash can and left that little restaurant as old friends again ... old friends in a new, deeper way.

When I got in the car, I didn't know whether to laugh or cry. I actually cheered. I praised God for this reconciliation, and thanked God for this friend. And now, as I write, I realize anew that our relationships with God go through similar phases sometimes. We aren't comfortable with each other. The conversation doesn't flow as well. We aren't sure we can trust as before—or we aren't sure we can be trusted as before.

At those tough times, I have learned that there is a lot to be said for just hanging in there. For keeping on going to church. For saying your prayers. For keeping the communication lines open. For sustaining your relationship on pure, stubborn commitment when all the warm feelings of affection seem gone forever. That kind of willpower, I am learning, is one of the purest forms of faith—a kind of faith you just don't develop until you are forced to, when your relationship with God seems to have gone bad. Sometimes faith means believing that doubt is just a stage, a rotten mood that will pass, and that in time, by the grace of God, you will get over it, and be old friends again in a new, deeper way.

Your Response

1. In what ways do I currently doubt against God?
2. In what ways do I currently doubt with God?
3. My plan for dealing with times of spiritual struggle:

Prayer

There are times, God, when I struggle in my faith. I may even become angry at you at times. It is childish, but I sometimes feel I need someone to blame for things I do not like, and you become the target for my anger. Help me not to become trapped in my anger. Thank you for the freedom to be honest about it. Thank you for being like an understanding parent to whom I can open my heart. I believe, but when I doubt, help me doubt with you and not against you, God.

Part 2

Help for the
Spiritual Search

Why Is Church the Last Place I Think of for Help in My Spiritual Search?

This chapter frankly acknowledges some of the difficulties in connecting with a church (or other faith community) for help on the spiritual journey. It suggests that there are three types of churches: Type 1 for "finders" or insiders only, Type 2 for "seekers" or the unconvinced only, and Type 3 for both "seekers" and the already-convinced. Finally, it suggests ten ways to get the most out of church.

Who Should Read This Chapter?

If you feel intimidated by or alienated from the church, this chapter is especially for you.

What Questions Does It Address?

Why should I consider connecting with a church, and what kind should I look for? How can I get the most out of church?

Two are better than one, because they have a good return for their labor: If they fall down, they can help each other up. But pity those who fall and have no one to help them up! Also, if two lie down together, they will keep warm. But how can one keep warm alone? Though one may be overpowered, two can defend themselves. A cord of three strands is not quickly broken.

Ecclesiastes 4:9–12

And let us consider how we may spur one another on toward love and good deeds, not giving up meeting together, as some are in the habit of doing, but encouraging one another.

Hebrews 10:24–25

No scientist could deny the importance of working within the conviviality and tradition of a community, from which he or she has learned the tacit skills of research through an implicit apprenticeship and to whose judgment the mature work is to be submitted for approbation or correction.... Those who speak of our being in a "post-modern" era frequently cite as one of its characteristics the recognition that community plays an important role in constituting our being.... These considerations provide a contemporary setting hospitable to the idea that ... the Church ... should find a place....

John Polkinghorne, *The Faith of a Physicist*

Because of piety's penchant for taking itself too seriously, theology—more than literary, humanistic, and scientific studies—does well to nurture a modest, unguarded sense of comedy. Some comic sensibility is required to keep in due proportion the pompous pretensions of the study of divinity.... This comes from glimpsing the incongruity of humans thinking about God.... The most enjoyable of all subjects has to be God, because God is the source of all joy. God has the first and last laugh. The least articulate of all disciplines [theology] deserves something in between.

Thomas C. Oden, *The Living God*

Postmoderns are not less interested in religion than ever before. Indeed, they are exploring new religious experiences like never before. The church has simply given them a less interesting religion than ever before.

Leonard Sweet, *Quantum Spirituality: A Postmodern Apologetic*

Why Is Church the Last Place I Think of for Help in My Spiritual Search?

Philip Yancey tells the story of a woman, a prostitute in Chicago, who found herself in "wretched straits, homeless, sick, unable to buy food for her two-year-old daughter." She came to a friend of Philip's:

> I could hardly bear hearing her sordid story.... At last I asked if she had ever thought of going to a church for help. I will never forget the look of pure, naïve shock that crossed her face. "Church!" she cried. "Why would I ever go there? I was already feeling terrible about myself. They'd just make me feel worse." (*What's So Amazing About Grace*, Grand Rapids: Zondervan, 1997, p. 11)

As a pastor, of course, I wince to hear these words, but I know she was right. Millions of people stay away from churches every week because they know that many if not most churches will more likely set them back than help them progress in their spiritual journey. Many of us are doing what we can to change that situation, but the fact remains: Church is often the last place people think of for help in their search for faith.

Church Names

You can learn a lot about churches by studying their names. For example, I was driving through the coastal plain of North Carolina a few days back and saw this huge sign, in a script reminiscent of the fireworks signs you also see in that part of the country: "Victry and Holiness Church of Our Lord Jesus Christ." The VAHCOOLJC church building itself appeared to be a converted Texaco station with a really bad paint job (white paint here, red paint there, all peeling, so you couldn't tell which came first). There were a few heroic plastic geraniums scraggling in oil drum planters (painted white) on the concrete islands where gas pumps once stood. It looked like the old garage was now the sanctuary, with the old office area serving as fellowship hall and Sunday school classroom. I assumed the restrooms were still restrooms.

The juxtaposition of the huge "Victry and Holiness" sign and the dwarfed, peeling, ramshackle Texaco station could probably become a metaphor for not just the VAHCOOLJC, but for every church of every denomination in every place. Because every community of faith—whether First Baptist, Fourth Presbyterian, Saints Andrew and Peter Roman Catholic, Beth Shalom Synagogue, or Fire Baptized Pentecostal Holiness Tabernacle—has high ideals and ethereal aspirations that make its actual accomplishments look by comparison like ... a run-down North Carolina gas station.

We all sneer at churches for how poorly they do in contrast to their high ideals. Love God? They can't even paint. Love one another? They can't even get together to plant real geraniums. Spread a saving message to the world? They can't even spell "victory." And we can go on and on—about how they spend money on cathedrals and neglect the poor, about the shameful way they treat homosexual people, about their racism and sexism, about the terrible way they forgot Uncle Bart when he was so sick and nobody even called or came to visit, and above all, about their bad taste in interior design. Sure, they have a few redeeming features. I'll bet you could get one heck of a potluck dinner at VAHCOOLJC, for example. And if you have to die, there is probably nobody better than the VAHCOOLJC choir to sing "Amazing Grace" at your funeral. But in spite of these small virtues, most of us find it easy to sneer at churches.

Enough Sneering!

Until you do what I did, that is. I got sick of myself and my friends sneering about churches, so we got together and started one. And guess what we found out? It's a whole lot harder than it looks. It's hard to raise money, and to get the musicians to show up on time, and to keep the Sunday school teachers getting along, and to remember to turn on the air-conditioning an hour early so the room is cool when everyone arrives (for hell hath no fury like overheated worshipers), and to keep the hand-clappers and the non-clappers from launching their own inquisitions against one another, complete with fiery tortures and heroic deaths. And if you succeed in doing those things — necessary things, if you want to have a church — you are run so ragged that it is hard to remember why you started the thing in the first place!

Here is what you find out: You find out that the higher our aspirations, the grander our ideals, the more sincerely we dream great dreams … the more paltry and pathetic our actual best accomplishments seem, grimy with old Texaco grease, faded like fake, sun-bleached geraniums.

The Other Side

And here is what else you find out: As paltry and pathetic as we seem, at least we try! At least we don't give up and live for the next sale at Kmart or Nordstrom! At least we keep the dreams alive! At least we try to get together, and get along, and grow in faith, and love each other, and honor God—even if it means we have to use the old Texaco toilets and sit on cold folding chairs! So, I salute the VAHCOOLJC! At least your sign stands big and bold! At least you hold your dreams! At least someone tried to spruce up that old shot Texaco station! At least someone had some vision! At least someone thought about and cared about victory and holiness, as opposed to mediocrity and sleaze! I would rather attend your grimy geraniumed garage than a beautifully landscaped country club with this sign out front: "Gathering of Comfortable, Apathetic People Who Stopped Dreaming and Growing and Who Feel Good Enough Just as We Are, Thank You."

Why You Should Find a Church

That is why, in spite of the notable failures of all our churches, I think you should find a community of faith if you are a sincere spiritual seeker. You are developing some spiritual dreams and aspirations of your own now, and you should band together with others who share them. Sure, you will have to put up with a lot. (And if you are human like the rest of us, you will give other folks some things to put up with too!) But perhaps that is one of God's tricks in the church. Just staying involved humbles us and teaches us patience, and those are good things for spiritual seekers to learn.

Now when I say this, some of you are probably thinking, "Wait. I am not ready for this yet. I am not even sure what I believe. You must be assuming I am farther along than I really am." No, I mean what I say, and I make no assumptions about where you are, as long as you are a sincere spiritual seeker. But I understand your concern. There are some kinds of churches that aren't ready for you, and you aren't ready for them either. That's why I recommend you find a community of faith that is a "Type 3."

Type 1 Groups

Type 1 groups are what we could call "finders only." The only people welcome there are people who already believe, who already agree, who already have found whatever it is that the current members have found. If you come in, not already agreeing, not already believing, you will be like a blue-jeaned and T-shirted teenager who shows up at a ritzy black-tie dinner party (or even worse, a middle-aged, tuxedo-clad, Bach-loving gentleman who shows up at a teenage bash). You—and everyone already assembled—will immediately know that you don't belong.

Type 1 churches are not bad, but they may be bad for you. How do you know if a house of worship is Type 1? Sometimes the name will tell you. If you can't figure out what the sign out front (or the ad in the Yellow Pages) means, it could be a sign that this place isn't right for you. (Sometimes, though, the sign out front has not changed, but the people inside have, and they will provide a warmer welcome for you than you might expect.) Better still, talk to someone who attends there. Ask, "Is this the kind of place that a person who doesn't already agree or believe will be welcome? Are you user-friendly for spiritual seekers?" People are surprisingly honest about this sort of question, and very often, rather than invite you into a disaster at their own church, they will graciously refer you elsewhere.

Type 2 Groups

Maybe you thought that all churches are Type 1, but fortunately, that is not the case. There are also Type 2 churches, which we could call "seekers only" churches. Type 2 faith communities are filled with people who are spiritual seekers of a sort. They would never sport a bumper sticker on their car that said, "I Found It!" or "Jesus is the Way!" or "Pray the Rosary!" or "Read the Koran!" or "Eat Kosher!" Type 2 churches attract the kind of people who are turned off by that kind of Type 1 dogmatism.

That is the strength of Type 2 churches—that anyone is welcome: atheist, agnostic, pantheist, monotheist, convinced, unconvinced. They are generally great places to go for intelligent discussion, freedom from dogma, open dialogue. But that can sometimes be their weakness too. If you are a spiritual seeker and you find something—if you begin to develop a more defined commitment to something or Someone specific, you may find yourself increasingly out of sync with a Type 2 faith community. The whole idea of these places is to be open to any ideas, and so any kind of significant closure and commitment can seem as unwelcome as the lack thereof would seem in a Type 1 group. In fact, Type 2 groups tend to attract people who have been burned in Type 1 groups. As such, they allow participants to keep up the social rhythms of church life—gatherings, music (even potluck dinners!), discussion on topics of ethics and spirituality and social justice—without the encroachment of anything too dogmatic.

Concerns

A Type 2 place would probably be more comfortable for you than a Type 1, but my main concern about a Type 2 is that it can easily turn your search into a destination. It can turn you from a seeker who is trying to find something to a seeker who is subtly pressured not to find anything. My additional concern with Type 2 groups is that you may not find much help there. If you are looking for a place to talk, to air your questions and frustrations, to dialogue, you will probably find that. But if you are looking for people who have themselves found something, people who have something going on in their lives beyond what you already have ... by definition, they may be hard to find. Even if they are there, they may be hesitant to talk openly about what they have found, because Type 2 churches generally aren't about finding. That is certainly not always the case. Some of the best-read and clearest-thinking people I have met belong to these kinds of faith communities. But the seek-and-don't-find problem is still worth monitoring.

Type 3 Groups

Type 3 groups, or "seeker-finder" groups, have the advantages of Type 2 churches—an accepting environment for people who don't already agree with their beliefs, morality, and so forth. They understand part of their mission as being there to help people like you in your search, and often they are very fluent in the language of your questions, doubts, objections, concerns, fears, hopes, and aspirations as a spiritual seeker. After all, many of them have just come down the same path you have as a sincere spiritual seeker.

Type 3 groups also have the advantages of Type 1 groups. Advantages? Yes, there are some. The challenge of explaining those advantages is one of my most difficult tasks in writing this book—difficult because I must use two despised words: tradition and dogma. I must try to convince you that tradition and dogma are not the same things as restriction and dogmatism. Here goes....

Imagine You are God

Let's imagine for a minute that you are God (silly, I know, but play along with me). And let's imagine that you (God) care a great deal about a sincere spiritual seeker by the name of _____ _____ (insert your name here). And let's imagine that you care no less for this spiritual seeker than you have for millions of others through the years. Let's imagine that your care is fatherly, motherly, which entails two things: first, that you don't have favorites, that you don't love one more than another qualitatively or quantitatively; and second, that you want your children not only to love you, but also to love one another.

In other words, imagine that your goal as God is not just to have individual, exclusive relationships with each of your children, but also that each of your children will have relationships with his or her siblings. Your goal is not to have a large number of isolated client relationships, but rather to have one interactive family relationship.

Let's imagine some of the reasons for desiring each seeker to be part of a larger family or community. First, since you (as God) are so much greater than each of your individual children, and since they are so limited, no one of them can know more than a sliver of you. But if they each share their unique perspectives, all can gain a broader experience of you. Not only that—but they will have a lot of fun together too.

Furthermore, there are many people in the family who have been seeking much longer than the new seeker. They would be equipped to help him find answers to many of his questions. They would also know better than the new seeker the spiritual pitfalls that all spiritual seekers face over time (and there are, as you probably have already found out, pitfalls aplenty). These more experienced family members would thus have much to teach the new seeker.

Now, still imagining you are God, you would have another concern. There are many spiritual realities that the new seeker has no idea of. He has no language for them, no experience of them. Take, for example, humility. The new seeker may know about humiliation, or self-effacement, or poor self-esteem ... none of which have anything in common with true humility as a spiritual virtue. Or take, for example, spiritual love, or charity. The new seeker may know about erotic love, friendship, affection, or team spirit, but spiritual love (which sees a stranger, or even an enemy, with the same tenderness as a lover) is a reality he only has the faintest concept of, if even that. He may have a PhD in biochemistry, awards in sales, credentials in CPR, and trophies in long-distance running, but in humility and charity he is a kindergartner, no, an infant.

And to make matters worse, he doesn't know how little he knows. He hears the words and thinks he knows, but he is ignorant even of his ignorance. If you are God, what do you do for him? He doesn't even have the language to learn what you want him to know. Might you want to put him into a community of people, into this family, which has been learning and preserving these virtues of humility and charity for centuries, so that he can see them demonstrated in real people, so he can see what he doesn't know and then begin to learn?

Now, still imagining you are God, let's extend the community even farther. What about the people who were part of this family a hundred years ago, a thousand years ago, and more? Would you want the wisdom and experiences of the past to be forgotten with each generation, or would you want them to be preserved in the family and passed on from generation to generation? In other words, would you want the new seeker to learn not only the lessons of his contemporaries, but also the accumulated wisdom of his forerunners through the centuries? Wouldn't the family history be important for him to learn and be a part of, for his benefit and also so that he can pass it on to the new seekers of tomorrow?

One more imagining: What if, through the centuries, the family has had some problems, some arguments? What if they developed misconceptions of you (as God) at times, imbalances, distorted images? And not only that, what if they developed some bad spiritual habits along with good ones at times, bad habits that needed to be corrected and avoided in the future? Wouldn't you want each new seeker to gain the benefit of the lessons learned from the mistakes of those who have gone before? Wouldn't you want him to know the skeletons in the family closet as well as the stories of the heroes and explorers?

A New Definition of Tradition and Dogma

Well, those accumulated stories, lessons, conclusions, embarrassments, celebrations, and memories are known as tradition and dogma. I know they have a bad name, and no doubt, it is one of the family embarrassments that people like me (pastors, preachers) have given them a bad name. You hear the words, and because of many people like me, you think: dogmatic, exclusive, unwilling to listen or dialogue, rigid, harsh, backward, outdated, arbitrary. But it doesn't have to be that way. To enter into the stories and lessons and heritage of a faith community can be exhilarating, exciting, liberating, educating.

Learning Math

Think about other things you have learned. Remember learning math? I remember the most terrible mistake I made in my math education: I got sick for two weeks with bronchitis when the class learned negative numbers. All of my education, I was taught, "You can't subtract a larger number from a smaller number." It was drilled into my head. But then, I was absent for two weeks, and when I came back, kids were at the blackboard, squeaky chalk in hand, breaking the rules—and the teacher didn't seem upset at all. It drove me crazy! Who was lying, the old teachers or the new one? Who changed the rules?

Eventually, my outrage calmed down. I realized that I had been given a provisional rule ("You can't subtract a larger number from a smaller one") that had been appropriate for a beginner like me, but the fact that I had obeyed it, as well as the other elementary rules, now meant that I was ready to graduate to a new set of rules. (Then came the letters. Why are they putting x's and y's in with those numbers? Then came the Greek letters. What are those S's and Q's doing here?)

No Independent Study

If the teachers had just given me a book and sent me off for "independent study," I couldn't have learned these new concepts on my own. For English, for social studies, I could do it on my own, but for math, I needed the teachers. Like my fellow students, at first, with each new concept, I didn't get it. I just did the problems, followed the instructions, listened to the explanations, blank-faced, brain-dead. It was all rote, memory, mechanical imitation, devoid of "getting it." But then, one by one, the concepts became my own; the lights came on. I "got them."

That is the real goal of tradition and dogma: not to impose a bunch of meaningless rules on you, not to oppress you or make you feel stupid, not to put you through meaningless exercises or assign "busywork" to keep you out of trouble, but to help you learn. The goal is for you to get it for yourself, so the lights will one day come on, so you can do work of your own: balance your own checkbook (negative numbers come in very handy there), figure out how much carpet to buy for your living room (how do you convert to square yards again?), build a bridge, design a spaceship to explore Mars.

A similar analogy could be made to learning music or painting or football. To learn, you must enter the tradition (Bach, Rembrandt, Vince Lombardi). You must master the dogma (key and time signatures, perspective, offensive strategy). You must associate with those who know more than you (music teachers, art teachers, coaches). The goal is not that you become a clone, but that you become a creative participant in the tradition—playing and composing and creating with your own style, contributing, receiving, and giving. You associate with the teachers and other students so that you can learn, know what they know, become like them, maybe even teach others someday, passing on the tradition and dogma yourself.

Tragic Failure

Sadly, many teachers of faith are even worse than the worst teachers of math, piano, painting, sports. How many kids hate math, despise piano, avoid art, have humiliating memories of sports because of those obnoxious "teachers" who should have been doing something else? The failure of religious educators is all the more tragic because the subject is so much more important. That is why (getting back to our main point) I think it's worth the effort to find the right community of faith. And that is why I think a well-led Type 3 group is the best to go for.

The search for God is in many ways a solitary search, but it cannot remain solitary. There comes a time to put down the books (including this one) and return from the lonely trail in the forest and meet the family, join the class, meet the teachers, join the community, learn the stories and lessons, past and present.

Where to Look

The greatest downside of Type 3 faith communities is their rarity. You can find them in nearly all denominations. (I won't say all, because some groups are firmly committed to a Type 1 or 2 approach.) I am glad to say that the number of Type 3 groups seems to be increasing. It is less a matter of the label on the front of the building and more a matter of the leadership (and hence the mission) of the individual community. But the problem remains: How do you find the Type 3 group that is right for you?

Here's a suggestion. Of all the people you know, think of the two or three whom you respect the most. Call, write, or email them, and explain to them: "I have begun some spiritual searching, and I am looking for a group that will help me in my search. Do you have any recommendations?" It might take some research. It might take several visits that are "no-go's." You might become so desperate that you will even pray and ask God to help you find the right group. (On second thought, don't wait until you are that desperate....)

Warnings

I can't go further without offering you some warnings. Although I believe you need a community of faith for your spiritual search to be authentic and effective, some churches will hurt your search more than they will help it. For example, some churches work like pyramid schemes, like the worst kind of network marketing, where there is a kind of euphoria each time a new "prospect" is brought in, and where everything seems to be done "for" the new prospect. But really, the new prospect is almost like food or fuel for the organization. Watch out for groups like these. If you are not wanted (as in many Type 1 groups), that's bad. If you are welcome and wanted (as in good Type 2 and 3 groups), that's good. But if you are needed in some unhealthy way, that's bad again.

Secondly, some groups, intentionally or unintentionally, can seek to impose a higher degree of pressure than is good for anyone, especially a sincere spiritual seeker like yourself. The pressure is counterproductive. On the one hand, if you yield to it, you develop (as we have seen) bad faith. On the other hand, if you resist it, you are both seeking and holding yourself back at the same time—an uncomfortable and frustrating posture to maintain for any length of time. Encouragement is good. Pressure is not.

Finding a good faith community is indeed an important component to finding good faith; just be sure to value the word "good," because an unhealthy group can be worse than no group at all. My quip a while back about praying for guidance in this regard is more important than it may have seemed. I have to believe that God will lead you to the group or groups you need, if you sincerely ask for guidance, knock on some doors, and enter the doors that are opened to you.

Getting the Most Out of Church

Once you are inside the door, I have several suggestions to help you get the most out of church.

1. Keep your expectations low. Don't expect to go from not getting negative numbers to getting calculus in one visit. Be realistic.

2. Keep your sense of humor. Reread the quote from Thomas Oden in the chapter preview, and remember VAHCOOLJC.

3. Expect to see weirdos. I visited a church with a friend recently. Wouldn't you know it, a fellow with an obvious mental illness—and an aversion to bathing—came and sat next to me. Through the whole service he mumbled to himself and smelled bad. My friend who invited me was, I think, quite embarrassed. I am sure my friend wanted to say, "Believe me, not everyone here is like the guy who sat next to you! This is actually quite a fine group of people!" And, of course, I knew that. The fact that they lovingly accepted this fellow showed me how fine they were. (There are a thousand other churches that talk about caring for the homeless, the needy, etc., etc., but have never actually made a smelly or mentally disoriented person feel as welcome in their midst as this guy clearly felt.) If churches are truly accepting, loving places, shouldn't we expect the rejected and unlovable to flock to them?

4. Expect to see hypocrites. In other words, expect the other people there to be about like you—imperfect, learning, with a long way to go, possessed by "victry and holiness" aspirations and achieving Texaco and geranium results.

5. Don't expect to like everything. The music might not match your tastes, and the speaker might have on an ill-fitting suit, and the carpet color may not match the curtains, and the lighting may be all wrong, and the pronouns may not be gender-inclusive. But that is not why you came. Try to get beneath all of that.

6. Listen to the words—the words of the songs, the sermon, the prayers—and plumb them for meaning. And be sensitive to the intangibles too: Do you feel anything special there? Do you get the feeling God shows up in this place?

7. Meet some people. Find some people you can relate to and ask for their names. Invite them over for coffee, or out for tennis, or something, anything, so you can build some relationships. Tell them exactly where you're coming from, why you're there: "Look, I am not a Christian (or Jew, or Moslem, or whatever) myself; I am on a kind of spiritual search, and I am hoping to find some help in my search here at your church (or synagogue, or mosque, or whatever)."

8. Ask them questions, direct questions: "Tell me about your spiritual background. Have you ever experienced God? Why do you believe as you do? What are the most important beliefs you hold? What advice would you have for someone like me? Would you pray for me?" Why beat around the bush? There are so many places where it's not "polite" to talk about religion or politics; take advantage of this place where religion is a safe topic! If they can't handle your questions, ask someone else, and if you can't find anyone at that church to help you, find another church.

9. Observe their relationships and lifestyles. Is it "good faith" that you are observing? Do the people love each other? Conflicts are inevitable with maturing, healing people like ourselves, so don't be surprised by conflicts—but do you see signs of grace: forgiveness, reconciliation, patience, understanding?

10. Get involved. Find a place you can volunteer. Don't just take: Give.

11. As you are able, participate in worship, prayer, service, fellowship, outreach. Obviously, you can't fake it. But as it comes, let it.

As It Comes, Let It

I have often wondered about the church, "God, couldn't you have done a better job than this? Couldn't you have suppressed hypocrisy more, allowed division and disunity less, edited (or prohibited) late-night religious television more, inspired better music and shorter sermons?" And the answer comes to mind: "Yes, but there would be no room for people like you." If God is going to let people like me in the church—people who learn slowly, who get manipulative when things don't quickly go their way, who lose their patience too quickly and too often, who have a lot to learn and a long way to go—then what's amazing isn't how many problems there are in churches, but rather that churches exist and function at all. It's amazing that all of our grit doesn't clog the gears; it's amazing that all of our viruses don't bring down the whole network. The farther along I go, the less I am surprised when things go wrong, and the more I am surprised when they go right for very long. It's a miracle, really.

These days I seem to be less scandalized by the distance between our reach and our grasp, between our idealistic signs and the faded, peeling realities they often represent. I find myself a little quicker to see the beauty, the wonder, the grace, and the genius in bringing people together into a humble community of faith where they need each other and where together they need God. Again, as that experience comes to you, let it.

Your Response

1. I would/would not like to find a faith community to help my search.
2. I would like to find a Type 1/2/3 faith community.
3. Here is a list of faith communities I would like to visit or revisit:
4. Here are the people who have most earned my respect, whom I might consult for referrals to a good faith community:
5. Here is how I plan to get the most out of my involvement with a faith community:

Resources

A good source for leads on Type 3 Christian churches is the Willow Creek Association, accessible via the internet at www.willowcreek.org. Another good source is www.emergentvillage.com. If you are interested in how churches can and must revitalize, you may be interested in my first book (now updated), *The Church on the Other Side.*

Prayer

God, I can't expect any faith community to be perfect. If it were, I couldn't join it without spoiling it. I do ask that you guide me to a faith community where you will help me grow and where you will use me to help others. I recognize that there are lessons I can learn and benefits I can receive in a faith community that I can gain nowhere else. I also feel a certain fear, because I am aware that I can become entangled or misled in many negative ways too. Again, in faith I ask you to guide me, and I will pursue involvement in a faith community with a posture of dependence on you.

Why Is the Bible the Next-to-Last Place I Think of for Help in My Spiritual Search?

This chapter acknowledges the difficulties faced by a modern reader approaching the Bible. It offers reasons to make use of the Bible as an important resource for spiritual growth, and then presents a brief summary of the Bible. It considers and rejects two common ways of approaching the Bible, and recommends a third approach.

Who Should Read This Chapter?

This chapter is especially for people who have never "gotten into" the Bible before.

What Questions Does It Address?

Why is the Bible so difficult for modern readers? Why does it come to us in the form it does? How can its problems actually be seen as advantages? What is the basic story of the Bible? How can the Bible be interpreted and applied intelligently today?

The Bible is not a kind of divinely guaranteed textbook in which we can, without any trouble, look up all the answers. I find the notion of the "classic," rooted in its own age but possessing through its underlying universality the power to speak across the centuries to other ages, to be the category which best contains my own understanding of the spiritual power of scripture.... It is the power of ... the Bible ... to speak freshly to each generation of its readers, revealing further truth, which becomes available, not by a process of alien imposition, but by the continuing elucidation of the profundity of the text.

John Polkinghorne, *The Faith of a Physicist*

Every part of Scripture is God-breathed and useful one way or another—showing us truth, exposing our rebellion, correcting our mistakes, training us to live God's way. Through the Word we are put together and shaped up for the tasks God has for us.

2 Timothy 3:16–17, *The Message*

Chapter 5

Why Is the Bible the Next-to-Last Place I Think of for Help in My Spiritual Search?

I have a confession to make: I have often wondered about the Bible, as I have about the church: "God, couldn't you have done better than this?" If God were trying to give us a holy book, a self-revelation, couldn't God have made it clearer, less controversial, more universal, less vulnerable to cultural irrelevancy? Couldn't there have been, instead of a collection of varied genres and wildly different writers living and writing in vastly different times and cultures, a single individual or committee inspired to give a coherent, chronological spiritual primer?

Instead of historically rooted books like "First and Second Thessalonians," "Psalms," or "Nehemiah," with mixtures of poetry, history, legislation, personal letters, and fiction, couldn't there have been clear, expository, timeless prose, with titles like, "First, Second, and Third Books of Theology," "The Truth About the Trinity," "How to Have a Good Marriage," "A Clear Guide to the End of the World," or "Seven Easy Steps to Cure Greed and Lust"? Couldn't God have anticipated every heresy, schism, problem, and controversy and made clear, unarguable, foolproof, preemptive strikes through some inspired chapter of a divine textbook?

What could God possibly think we gain by having a collection of holy Scriptures in this seemingly disorganized, patchwork form, if indeed they come from God at all?

After my mind follows this train of thought for a while, I begin to ask a different question: How else could it be? If God is indeed having a real story unfold through history, then of course, the story has to "happen" with freedom, and the reports of it have to come to us in their raw, unedited forms, warts and wrinkles, bizarre twists and unpredictable turns. And even if God were to edit the stories into a more "acceptable" form, for which audience would God edit them? For scientific, college-educated rationalists? For wild-eyed artists and poets? For rice farmers in the East, fishermen in the North, hunter-gatherers in the South, or philosophers in the West? For gender-egalitarians from the West (guaranteeing it wouldn't be read by more patriarchal folk from some other places), or vice versa? Would it really be better for us to have the story rehashed and "sanitized" so we like it more readily and accept it more easily? Or is there some benefit to getting it gritty, breathless, and warm from the lips of those who were there, told in their idioms, through the lenses of their cultures—leaving the job of interpretation and application for our myriad and dynamic settings up to us?

If God wants us to interact personally with the story, to go deep with it, so that it captivates and inspires and transforms us, then of course, it must offer challenges, mysteries, amazements, bafflements—not just journalistic clarity or technical precision. If it describes astounding, shocking realities (visions, miracles) experienced only a few times in history, how could there be easy language and common metaphor that would render the unexplainable as explainable, the uncommon as pedestrian? No wonder parts of it are unheard-of, bizarre. If God wants it to be a book that interests and challenges people around the globe for their whole lives, that guides us into life's deep mysteries, that trains us to see the world from diverse points of view and in so doing, stretches us to not be so limited by our own inherited point of view, then of course it can't be like the phone book, a government code, or a high school biology textbook — easy reference, fully indexed, conveniently formatted for quick, easy use.

Nor can it be a one-read book, after which we say, "The Bible? Oh, yes, I read that years ago," implying that we will never need to look at it or think about it again. If God wants the book to be an authentic medium of spiritual enlightenment and instruction, then how can it be a book that we feel we can fully grasp, have control over, take pride in our knowledge of, feel competent in regards to? Mustn't it be an untamed book that humbles us, that entices us higher up and deeper in, that renders us children rather than experts, that will sooner master us than we will master it?

If the book isn't only to be about God, but also about us ... not only revealing the Creator, but also contributing to the formation of a family, a movement, a heritage, then mustn't it have our fingerprints on it, showing us not only God but ourselves in relationship with God and one another? And if God is interested in recording an unfolding story in such a way as to foster its continued unfolding, without so explaining and clarifying it that the story is spoiled, bled of its drama, de-plotted, demystified ... then wouldn't the book you would expect look very much like the book we actually have?

Cantankerous Form

Might its cantankerous form tell us that there are things more important in life than a good, logical, linear outline? That we are more than brains ... that we have imagination, passion, fury, hope ... and that God is as interested in converting and informing these as our conceptual selves? Might it tell us that all contact with God (at least for us humans, and for now) must be situational ... that there is no way for us to know God except in the ways that people in the Bible story did: in the middle of feast and famine, good and bad governments, changing economies, disappointing marriages and dysfunctional families, poignant moments and exhilarating victories, deep friendships and bitter betrayals?

And might it have a built-in security system, so the insincere or halfhearted find nothing, so the prejudiced find exactly what they were expecting, and so those who are hungry and thirsty for God find a spiritual feast?

So, I complain less about the Bible these days, and appreciate it more, without asking it to be something else, which would, I now realize, be something less. And I encourage everyone I can not to bypass the Bible, but rather to dive into it with gusto, for it provides amazing resources for those on a spiritual journey.

The Five-Minute Bible Survey

If you are not familiar with the Bible, let me offer this brief overview. The Bible is a collection of ancient "books," or documents, which together become the basic library of monotheism on planet earth. The thirty-nine (or twenty-four, depending on which are grouped together) documents that comprise the Hebrew Bible cover a period from roughly 2000 BC until about 450 BC. To them are sometimes added fifteen more documents (or thirteen, depending again on which are grouped together) which are often called the "Apocrypha," and which cover the period from about 300 BC to AD 100. Christians include twenty-seven more documents, together called the "New Testament," covering a period from just before the birth of Christ to about AD 65–90.

These documents include history, poetry, prophecy (messages from God in specific situations, sometimes, but not all that often really, predicting the future), and personal letters. Within these genres, there are numerous clear examples of fiction—parables, dreams, and so forth. Sometimes it's hard to tell exactly what a passage is intended to be—history, poetry, fiction, nonfiction.

All of these documents combine to communicate a story, a beautiful story, a haunting story, a nearly unbelievable but, to many of us, ultimately believable story. Let me try to summarize it for you.

The Story

Before the beginning of everything we think of as "the universe," there was God—a creative (as God was soon to prove), intelligent, conscious, communicating, dynamic, caring entity whose magnitude goes beyond our limits both of perception and imagination. God created the universe, using time, space, matter, energy ... and something more. When God created our planet and populated it with life, God chose to insert something of his own self into the mix: into human beings, God would breathe his own "breath of life," his very Spirit, his own image.

This mysterious endowment was a great ennoblement, but it brought with it a certain burden, a responsibility unknown to granite or paramecia, mushrooms or sequoias, bog turtles or crocodiles, seagulls or sparrows, otters or gorillas. That unique endowment and responsibility made the first humans—and us, today—capable of freedom, wisdom, creativity, love, communication, civilization, virtue; it also made them vulnerable to rebellion, pride, foolishness, destructiveness, hatred, division, and vice. They, as we, too often fell to the latter.

So, being neither robots nor prisoners, these free human beings early on failed to fulfill the full promise of their primal innocence and natural nobility, and with the development of the first civilizations it was clear that human beings had a self-destructive bent. One feature of their self-destructiveness was their tendency to lose contact with God, to live life without reference to God, to throw away their spiritual compass and get lost. That didn't mean they became irreligious; in fact, they seemed incurably religious, incapable of numbing or obliterating their spiritual faculties, at least not for very long. Rather, their estrangement from their Creator meant that they innovated as best they could, developing religions as varied as their cultures and their landscapes. In fact, by about 2000 BC, each social entity on earth had developed its own religion to explain its mysteries, solve its problems, bolster its power, vilify its enemies, and so on. The assumption on planet earth was that there were many gods, each having power over certain territories or certain natural phenomena (the sun, the moon, fertility). Some of their forms of worship were no doubt beautiful and honorable, but many became base and degrading—including horrific human sacrifice, sexual exploitation, and the like.

A Family with a Destiny

Into this situation of religious pluralism, with a welter of religions mixing beauty and horror, truth and misunderstanding, the Creator communicated with a Semitic shepherd living in modern-day Iraq, then known as Chaldea. The man's name was Abram, later known as Abraham. Abraham was given a sense of destiny, that he would be the father of a great family, and that his descendants would bring spiritual blessing and enlightenment to the whole world. Key to this enlightenment was this revelation: There were not many gods, but only one. And this God could not be adequately represented by any of the standard images (idols), but was greater than the stars and the sea, more majestic than the sky and the mountains, because all things were created by this God. Not only that, but this God was deeply concerned about the ethics, morality, social justice, and personal integrity of human beings, himself being ethical, moral, just, and pure. (What a contrast to the capricious god-concepts of Abraham's neighbors, gods whose vices were as exaggerated as their powers!)

These were radical ideas, though they may seem common-place to us (which is proof of Abraham's influence!). They took generations to embed in their shared understanding. But God was patient; these creations were made to be free, so they could not be pushed or forced. They had to learn at their own pace, so direct intervention (via some extraordinary spiritual experience—a vision, a voice, a dream) was always delicate. Additional interventions came, though, at critical times, to Abraham's son Isaac, Isaac's son Jacob (who was later renamed Israel, this name becoming the "family name" of the Jewish people to this day), and Jacob's son Joseph. The family was guided to a land of their own just east of the Mediterranean, where this new understanding of God could be nurtured in relative peace and stability. But it would take a difficult experience to solidify their identity and more deeply root these new beliefs in this family of people, and through them, in the human family as a whole.

United in Suffering

A famine drove them from their land to Egypt, where they would either assimilate into Egyptian culture and squander their destiny or intensify their distinct family identity as refugees, and not only as refugees, but eventually, as an oppressed, enslaved minority group as well. These shared sufferings did their work, and after about four hundred years in Egypt, their identity survived, their spirit was still (barely) unbroken by their hardships, and their unique faith in one supreme God remained embedded deeply within them. God intervened again, calling a uniquely prepared man named Moses to liberate these special people from their oppression and enslavement and return them to their homeland, which had been unseen by them for four centuries.

The return took much longer than one might expect, because the land could not be resettled by halfhearted followers. During this difficult but formative time, the family wandered as nomads in the harsh wilderness between Egypt and Palestine. It was during this nomadic period (called the Exodus) that formal public worship of God began. Additionally, the moral standards of this community of faith became codified during these years, most notably in the Ten Commandments. No wonder Moses is remembered as such an important figure in the family history of the Jewish people, since he led the people through this amazing passage.

Conquest, Confederacy, and Kingdom

A generation later, a reinvigorated younger generation completed the conquest (because other tribes had moved into the land during their absence) of their homeland. The extended family now consisted of twelve clans, and they formed a loose confederacy that was frequently challenged by neighboring nations, sometimes overcome, and subsequently reformed several times over the next several hundred years.

Eventually, this loose confederacy evolved into a rather short-lived monarchy, a development about which later biblical writers were ambivalent. Their first king, Saul, was a disappointment. Their heroic second king, David, initiated their "golden age," around 1000 BC. His son Solomon was another disappointment as a king, and Solomon's son was such a weak and insecure ruler that civil war broke out, and the nation was divided into northern and southern kingdoms.

Deterioration, Exile, Return

Into this deteriorating situation, the people continued to experience God. Sometimes, God gave people strong dreams and vision to get their attention. Occasionally, remarkable miracles occurred. Some people were given a special sensitivity to God and became spiritual leaders called prophets. Their writings in the Bible record the context and content of the messages they received from God and passed on to the people.

In this divided and weakened condition, the descendants of Israel became an easy target for rising empires to their north and east. Eventually, from about 700 to 550 BC, both the northern and southern kingdoms were conquered. Many survivors from the south were deported to Babylon where they became servants in various capacities. Seventy years later, two leaders, Nehemiah and Ezra, gained permission to repopulate their homeland and led the refugees (most of whom had been born in exile) back to rebuild their capital city, Jerusalem.

Through all these hardships, these people never completely lost faith. Nor did they allow their faith to lose its distinctiveness.

Of all people in the world, they alone believed in one supreme, good Creator, and they sought to remain faithful to that vision. The era of the great Hebrew prophets ends with the story at this point, about 450 BC.

A New Chapter

During the next 450 years, the Greek empire flourished and the Roman empire rose, subjugating the Jewish people as they did the whole Mediterranean world. The Jewish people showed inspiring courage and faithfulness to God during these times of political and religious persecution. Many stories of their courage and faith are contained in the Apocrypha, which comes from this period. Into this milieu was born Jesus, later to be called the Christ, meaning the Messiah or Savior or Deliverer. After thirty years of obscurity, Jesus came into the public eye, presenting himself as an itinerant Jewish rabbi and prophet ... with a difference. The religious world of his day was polarized — much as ours is — between various factions that had different approaches to politics, economics, and spirituality.

Jesus refused to be contained in any of their boxes. He said that a time of change had come, a new chapter was beginning, a whole new era in the spiritual life of the human race was being launched. With the memory of the great golden age of King David far behind them (far, but not forgotten), and with the oppressive grandeur of the Roman kings around them ... Jesus announced a new kingdom, the kingdom of God.

Upside Down

Everything about this kingdom was upside down. In it, the poor and meek were winners, not the rich and aggressive. In it, some prostitutes and tax collectors were far ahead of many priests and Pharisees. Children and women were given unheard-of status, and God was brought nearer than ever before: Jesus said that in this new era of the kingdom of God, God could be known as a loving, caring, compassionate father ... and that even rebellious runaways would be warmly welcomed home.

The crowds flocked to hear this message. Reports of miraculous healings were commonplace, although Jesus himself tried to keep them quiet. Naturally, the religious establishment felt threatened, and so they conspired with the Roman authorities to have Jesus arrested and killed. Their plot succeeded through the help of an insider, one of Jesus' twelve prime students (called disciples), and one Friday afternoon, Jesus was crucified and buried.

Surprises

Three days later, reports began to spread that the tomb where Jesus had been placed was now empty, and that Jesus had risen from the dead. At first, not one of the disciples believed these rumors, but in the coming days, one by one and in larger groups, they claimed to have encounters with the risen Jesus. For two thousand years the descendants of Abraham had — more or less successfully — guarded their faith, kept their distinctiveness, monitored their faithfulness, resisted continuous pressures to culturally conform, adopt the religious practices of other nations, or in any way allow their unique commitment to monotheism to be polluted or diluted. Isolation, separation, distinction were at the core of their being. And now, the disciples report, Jesus is telling them to bring the good news of this new kingdom to the entire world, to every nation, every religion, every culture, every language. Further, they came to understand that Jesus' death had not been a colossal accident, but rather was part of God's plan: In some mysterious way, as Jesus suffered and died, he was absorbing and absolving the wrongs of the whole human race, and demonstrating a new kind of power, a new way of bringing peace and reconciliation. Now, the whole human race could receive forgiveness and reconciliation with God and one another; it would be as simple as asking, seeking, believing, and entering an open door.

Still Unfolding Today

If Jesus was right, then the one true God wasn't just for the descendants of Abraham anymore. Belief in, relationship with, and experience of the one true God was to permeate the whole world, like yeast slowly rising in bread, or like seeds subtly planted in the soil. The time had come to open the doors to everyone. There would be a thousand problems, Jesus said. It would be messy, with plenty of mistakes and no shortage of opposition. It would take time, a long time. But they should not give up until every person hears the "good news" — that God loves them all, wants to welcome them into his family, and wants to involve them in the ongoing spiritual story of the human race.

The New Testament concludes with the story of the spread of that message and the creation of faith communities all over the Mediterranean world. And that story continues to unfold today. Perhaps, as you read and I write, we are part of its unfolding even now.

Interpreting the Story

Now when it comes to interpreting this story, when people read the Bible and try to discern what it means to our lives and situations today, there are two common approaches, neither of which I will recommend to you.

1. The literalist approach requires us to take the Bible literally from beginning to end. If by literally we mean, literally "paying attention to every letter," well, okay. That's what good readers do anyway. But if by literally we mean unimaginatively, without regard to the many different genres represented in the Bible or the many different cultural backgrounds of the original writers, treating the whole thing like a code of law or textbook on science, prying the Bible out of its milieu, pretending to unjustified levels of certainty ... I am sorry, I can't recommend that.

2. The liberal approach — rightly, I believe — distances itself from the wooden reading of the worst literalists. But I believe many liberals overreact. They do not wish to be bound by the outmoded worldviews of the past — whether from Abraham's time, David's time, or Jesus' time — so they sometimes take the Bible and subject it to the worldview of our own time. Whatever seems distasteful to contemporary ears doesn't pass through their grid. In so doing, they become slaves to our contemporary culture (which, a hundred or thousand years from now, will seem as backward and silly as any past worldview seems to us). That leaves them just as parochial as any literalist, stuck in the worldview or plausibility structure of today just as literalists may be in their alternative worldview from the past.

Both literalists and liberals find various ways to downplay uncomfortable elements in the Bible (for some, stories of miracles, limitations on sexual behavior; for others, calls to economic equity or peacefulness). They find ways to ignore some parts of the Bible's message, perhaps ridiculing them as primitive and silly, or perhaps using sophisticated arguments to blunt their impact. In any case, what's left is a domesticated Bible, a "nice"

Bible, a tame Bible that, I fear, presents a God and world redesigned in our image.

A Third Option?

Could there be a third approach? I think so. Let me outline it like this:

1. Let's begin by accepting the idea that God wants to speak to us through the Bible. It contains the story of the romance between God and humanity, and our fellow spiritual travelers for centuries have felt that it is profitable for our spiritual health and development. To lightly discard it would be at least unwise, and probably arrogant too. We would soon find ourselves in deep weeds indeed, without it.

2. Let's continue by acknowledging that we need the Bible. We need to know the story, we need to learn from the sages of the past, we need the benefit of their experiences and mistakes, we need the inspiration. We need the corrective perspectives given in the Bible, vantage points from outside our contemporary culture (which is so natural to us that we are unaware of how it may limit or distort our perceptions), foreign vantage points from which to view ourselves, distant fulcra upon which to get leverage to move ourselves in better directions.

3. Let's also frankly acknowledge that certain things in the Bible present problems to us. For example ...

   A. Does the Bible really require us to believe that the earth was created in 144 hours, something less than 10,000 years ago?
   B. Does the Bible allow only male-dominated social or ecclesiastical structures? Is patriarchy the only biblically permissible mode for society?

C. Does the Bible recommend sanctions against homosexual people, and if so, what sanctions, and why?

D. Does the Bible require us to believe that anyone who doesn't believe it in its entirety is going to hell after death, and if not, which parts can one be ignorant of or skeptical about, and why?

4. Let's avoid the extreme responses of both literalists and liberals, the one refusing to reconsider their interpretations of the Bible in light of contemporary experience, and the other refusing to reconsider contemporary biases and "certainties" in light of the Bible. In other words, let's try to practice good faith in the Bible, refusing to deny either our own experience on the one hand or our respect and need for the Bible on the other. Where we can't reconcile contemporary experience and the Bible, we can honestly admit that we just don't know, having confidence that we will be led in time to better understanding. We can live in that dynamic tension, make the best of it, and be gracious to one another in the meantime.

5. Let's spend a minority of our time and energy on the controversies, and concentrate fully on the biblical teachings that are clear and compelling without debate. Mark Twain said as much: It wasn't the parts of the Bible that he didn't understand that bothered him — but the parts he did understand. For example, it is pretty clear that what is most important in life is for us to love God with all our heart, soul, mind, and strength, and to love our neighbors as ourselves. Our personal spiritual health and the contemporary unfolding of the biblical story will both fare better, I think you'll agree, if we concentrate for the next twenty-five years on those simple, clear basics. Somehow, I can't help but think the other issues will fall into place over

time. Jesus chided the Bible scholars of his day for "straining out a gnat and swallowing a camel." Ironically, whether liberal or literalist, we could easily do the same thing, concentrating so on the minor controversies that we miss the big picture.

My Experience with the Bible

I have spent most of my adult life as a pastor, so I have been constantly interacting with the Bible in my own personal thinking and in preparation for the next week's sermon. At least forty-five times each year for twenty-four years, I prepared and presented a new message from the Bible for the church I served. And now, as an author and traveling speaker, I do the same thing—just for different crowds each week. people often ask me, "Don't you ever run out of things to say?" I tell them, "No, I wish I could preach several times each week. There's always more to say. This book is so rich!" Week after week, year after year, I see the relevance, power, resources, and wisdom of this book. It really is amazing.

Many of the people who come to the church I serve (which, as you probably have guessed, is what we earlier called a Type 3 church) don't believe in the Bible when they come. They are skeptical. I don't tell them they have to believe it. I just try to present it. I try to be honest about the parts that confuse me. I try to focus on the parts that are abundantly clear and profitable (and I am quite certain that my lifetime will end before I reach the last of those things!). And over time, I notice that people come to share my respect for and trust in the Bible—as a needed, dependable, enlightening, unique, challenging, fascinating resource for spiritual seekers ... a book with God's fingerprints all over it and his breath behind the words.

Your Experience with the Bible

There are many ways you can interface with the Bible. You can read it on your own. You can use a self-study guide. You can join a Bible study group or class. You can attend a church where the Bible is the basis for the sermons. There are Internet chat rooms oriented to Bible study and telephone hotlines where you can call with your questions. You will find several resources in the appendix to help you get into the Bible in a productive way.

Pointing Outward

As wonderful as the Bible is, it doesn't seem to intend its own function to be like that of television: Watch more and more, stay on the couch for another thirty minutes, never turn it off, why go outside? Don't change that channel; don't go away! No, the Bible seems to keep sending you away ... to think, to live, to feast, to fast, to meet, to serve, to stand firm, to back down, to confront, to apologize, to worship, to teach, to learn, to love. And before long, you have new reasons to come back, new questions, new predicaments, new needs ... through which you will find new adventures into which you will be sent away, and so on. It is the life that counts, not the reading about it. The book is there to thrust you into life, again and again chasing you off the couch, challenging you into new adventure.

Your Response

1. I would describe my experience with the Bible as

nonexistent
negative
positive
mixed

2. My approach to the Bible will be

   literalist
   liberal
   third alternative
   other

3. I would like to

   begin reading the Bible on my own
   join a Bible study group
   other

4. I will be reading the Bible for the following purposes,
   or to find answers to the following questions:

Resources

Many people these days have benefited from getting the Bible on audiotape, so it can be listened to during commutes, exercise, or other activities.

Several films depict Jesus' life, with more or less accuracy. The *Jesus* film produced by Campus Crusade for Christ is one of the best, as is *Jesus of Nazareth* (directed by Franco Zeffirelli).

If you are one of the many people put off by the Bible and its vocabulary, you shouldn't miss Kathleen Norris's *Amazing Grace: A Vocabulary of Faith*. Norris tackles what were to her offensive biblical and theological words like sinner, salvation, blood, dogma, and orthodoxy, and shares how she got through the offense to meanings that have enriched her faith. As well, my books *The Story We Find Ourselves In* and *A Generous Orthodoxy* may be of help—the former in presenting the big picture of the biblical story and the latter in addressing some difficulties people have with the Bible.

Many churches offer Bible study groups. As you get involved in a community of faith, these can be an excellent resource.

If I were to recommend a short syllabus of Bible reading, it would be Genesis 1–3, selected Psalms (1, 8, 19, 23, 27, 32, 51, 95, 150), Isaiah 40–53, the gospel of Luke, and Colossians 1–4.

Prayer

God, I would be arrogant and unwise to shun the insights of sages and leaders from the past whose reflections on having a relationship with you have been authenticated through the ages. So I do not want to ignore the rich heritage of monotheism on planet earth found in the Bible. But, God, I confess that the Bible is often difficult for me; I feel so far removed from the ancient world, its languages, customs, and culture. Help me bridge these gaps and not be distracted by secondary matters; help me to see the truth you have for me in the Bible. Let it be a mirror to help me better see myself and a light to help me progress on this path of spiritual searching and growth. I don't want to just keep learning and thinking; I want to put my faith into practice in my daily life.

What If I Lose Interest?

This chapter faces the real possibility of losing interest in the spiritual search. It uncovers a factor in many if not all people that may sabotage the spiritual search. It summarizes both costs and benefits of staying with the spiritual journey long term. The chapter concludes with a brief consideration of hell and heaven as ultimate factors in a cost-benefit analysis.

Who Should Read This Chapter?

Anyone planning on long-term spiritual growth should give this chapter a careful reading.

What Questions Does It Address?

Why might we be tempted to suppress the truth or in other ways sabotage or abandon our own spiritual search? What are the costs and corresponding benefits that will make persevering worthwhile? What are the purposes of the horrific imagery of hell and the beautiful imagery of heaven in religious literature?

But even as hope died in Sam, or seemed to die, it was turned to a new strength. Sam's plain hobbit-face grew stern, almost grim, as the will hardened in him, and he felt through all his limbs a thrill, as if he was turning into some creature of stone and steel that neither despair nor weariness nor endless barren miles could subdue.

J. R. R. Tolkien, *The Return of the King*

What If I Lose Interest?

Grace and I have four children. In 1990, Trevor, our third child, was six years old ... a wonderful, thoroughly normal (and thoroughly extraordinary, too, of course) kid. Then he got cancer.

His regimen of chemotherapy kept his immune system next to nonfunctional. This immuno-compromised state meant that any infection was potentially life-threatening. Seven times in the first nine months of treatment, he would spike a fever, we would have to rush him to the hospital, and he would spend a few days or weeks there on intravenous antibiotics.

Turtles

One of his infections was identified as salmonella. That was a haunting diagnosis for me to hear, because I had an unusual hobby: I kept and bred rare turtles and tortoises, animals which sometimes carry salmonella. The natural question: Did my son catch this infection from my animals? If the antibiotics couldn't fight it, and (perish the thought) Trevor died, would my hobby have cost my son his life? How could I forgive myself? How could my wife forgive me?

Of course, the infection could have come from other sources, and we never found out the actual source. Early on in treatment, Trevor developed a craving (another side-effect of his chemotherapy) for eggs, and several times we found him in the kitchen in the middle of the night scrambling or poaching some eggs: "I was just hungry, Mom and Dad. I didn't want to wake you up." Perhaps he got salmonella from the eggs—from undercooking them, or from failing to wash his hands after touching the raw eggs. But the possibility was there that his infection was from the turtles, and therefore *my fault*. Can you imagine how this thought haunted me during his entire hospitalization?

Pressure-treated Lumber

Not only that, but another fear plagued me. When Trevor was younger, I had built a loft bed for him and his big brother. The only problem was this: I used pressure-treated lumber to make the bed. I was basically ignorant of the danger of the chemicals in the wood at the time. Some time later, I learned that this lumber should never be used indoors, or anywhere it will have frequent contact with human skin—because the chemicals used to treat the wood can be carcinogenic.

Even then, when someone told me of the danger, it took me several months before I got around to dismantling the bed and disposing of the wood. Cancer seemed like such a far-off risk. There was no urgency.

Looking back, I am horrified and deeply ashamed of my carelessness on both counts—choosing the wrong materials and taking my time about removing them. The results could have been fatal. Some months after Trevor's diagnosis, I remember the thought sending a shiver up my spine: "I may be the cause of his disease, his suffering."

"You didn't mean it," you might say. "You weren't trying to give him cancer. It wasn't intentional." True, but carelessness is carelessness, and unintentional carelessness can kill as effectively as intentional malice. In my own soul, I know this is true. I shouldn't have taken any chances with my son's health, in one case with letting that bed stay in the house for even one night after I heard that it was dangerous ... and in the other case by allowing in our home a possible threat of needless infection for my immuno-compromised son. I am ashamed to have to admit these failures, but they happened.

Why Dredge This Up?

Thank God, Trevor survived all his infections—including salmonella—and he has been cancer-free for many years now, as good as cured, the doctors say. Why am I dredging up these terrible memories, then? Everything turned out okay, so why not drop the whole thing?

Because of this: In both cases, I was strongly tempted to suppress this truth. I am also ashamed to have to admit this, but I didn't want to let the doctors know about my turtle hobby, and I didn't want to admit the possible role of the loft bed in causing my son's disease. I wanted to let everyone assume it was chicken eggs, or to know nothing of pressure-treated lumber in the house. I wanted to protect myself. I wanted to deny any possible culpability.

Two Implications

My desire to suppress the truth, to protect myself, to cover up my mistakes—if it has some corresponding reality in you, and if it is in fact indicative of a problem common to all of us—has at least two frightening implications regarding our search for faith and for God:

1. We may not really want to find God.
2. We may not want to find the real God.

In other words, we need to acknowledge that just as there are spiritual hungers and thirsts in us, moving us along in our search, there are contrary forces and fears that will vote every chance they get to back-burner the search, abandon it altogether, or in some other way compromise its integrity. For that reason it is wise to ask ourselves some questions.

Fake Searching

What if deep inside, we know that God is all about truth (the whole truth)? And what if we feel guilty about things we have done, are doing, or would like to do? What if we would like the truth about ourselves — our carelessness, our deceit, our worst secrets — to be suppressed? Wouldn't that give us every reason to not want to find or face God? Might it tempt us to conduct a false search, where we pretend to want faith, but really are just going through the motions — so as not to look guilty? Wouldn't that state of affairs make God the enemy, paradoxically the one we seek and the one we seek to avoid?

What if we have some cherished vices? What if we nurture secret lives that we are deeply ashamed of, dark sides to our psyche that would scandalize everyone we know if they were known? What if there are sexual affairs, secret perversions, shady business practices, well-covered addictions, or sweet bitternesses embedded in our hearts like thorns in our thumbs? And what if, partway through our search, we begin to sense that God wants to deal with those things ... that coming to him will require us to come to ourselves, come into the light so to speak, come clean about these secrets? Will that fear tempt us to abort our search? When pushed to the wall, will we decide we love shadows rather than light, our pet pleasures more than spiritual authenticity?

Will we conveniently lose interest right at the point we most need to press on?

Respectability

It might not be such ugly things. It might be more "respectable" things—like respect itself. Maybe people think of you as a certain kind of person ... independent, fiercely nontraditional, iconoclastic, rigorously logical, cool, detached. Maybe they respect you for those qualities. To "come out of the closet" as a person of faith would blow that image, force you to eat some of your skeptical words of the past, require you to admit that you were wrong before, humble you to admit that you needed something beyond yourself after all.

I remember this feeling. I was a teenager when I went through a critical phase in my spiritual journey. I remember feeling, with some excitement, "It's happening! My faith is coming alive! God is really real after all! This is wonderful! I can't wait to tell people about this!" Then a wet blanket descends: "But I am already the president of the church youth group. What will they think if I tell them it's just coming together for me? Will they think I have been a hypocrite? Well, actually, they would be right. But do I want them to know it? Maybe I shouldn't admit this transformation I am experiencing. Maybe I should just pretend that this newfound faith had been there all along...."

Counting the Cost

Do you see the trap? If I capitulate to the fear of losing people's respect, if I begin to pretend, if I perpetuate a fraud, then I turn my good faith into bad faith, and I basically guarantee that I am not going any further in the development of good faith. This search for faith ends up being pretty costly.

I need to be straight with you in this regard. I need to repeat that previous statement: Faith ... good faith, real faith ... can be pretty costly. A person finding faith sooner or later has to count the cost. He will either lose interest and turn back at that point or forge ahead. Generally, as you would expect, the greatest breakthroughs often follow those decisions to pay the price and plunge onward, in spite of the cost.

Costs

Let's assess some of the costs that often accompany spiritual growth:

1. *Pride.* At some point, no, at many points, you will have to learn how deep your pride's roots go. Like a gardener facing a weed-choked flower bed, you will feel the agony of uprooting egotism, arrogance, conceit, selfishness. Probably all of the following debits in our "cost of faith" list are simply line items in the pride account.

2. *Judgmentalism.* Good faith requires you to face your own failures, which increasingly makes it seem morally obscene to be so hard on other people. Good faith requires you to say good-bye to judgmentalism and all her clones: racism, sexism, agism, classism, holier-than-thou-ism, and all of their arrogant ism-counterparts, because faith requires you to acknowledge (not just to say, because nearly everybody says this without really meaning it) that you are ultimately no better than anybody else.

3. *Vices.* In the past, you could always judge yourself by other people, and there were always copious quantities of worse people around who, by their very badness, inadvertently did you the favor of helping you feel superior. As you move into faith,

though, you stop comparing yourself favorably to others, and start comparing who you are to the person you could be, the person God wants you to become. Indulgences you used to allow yourself now seem cheap, beneath you, dangerous spiritually, dangerous to others even, because of the negative example they set. It's not that you are being forced to give up anything; it's that certain things don't fit anymore, like last decade's styles (wide ties, narrow ties, paisley socks, polyester, whatever ...) — you could wear them, but they are just not "you" anymore.

4. *Imbalance.* Without good faith, you can afford to be a workaholic or a slacker. You can obsess on golf or sex, antiques or danger. You can be a rabid Republican or a demonic Democrat. You can be a miser or a prodigal, flighty or stodgy, overdose on privacy or parties. Choose your extreme; choose your imbalance ... anything is open for you. But as good faith becomes more part of your life, as God becomes more part of your life, you start to desire balance.

5. *Apathy.* Apart from faith, you can indulge your apathy by saying, "Why try anything new? Why work for a better world? Real improvement is impossible. What difference can I make anyway?" Enter faith, and a whole new factor enters the equation. Words like "impossible" seem out of place. Despair and cynicism feel like insults to God. Hope grows, and love, and therefore motivation to care, to give, to act, to try, to dream, to risk.

6. *Greed.* "What's mine is mine, and I want to keep it," we say before we have faith. We might even go further: "What's yours is mine, and I want to take it ... and who's going to stop me?" After faith, we change: "What's mine is really God's, and so I want to use it as God would want me to use it — for my needs, for others' needs, as God wills."

Obviously, our list could extend well beyond these six, but they fairly represent the kinds of costs that go along with faith, costs you must sooner or later assess and decide to either forego or pay in full. Don't face them, and you will lose interest in your spiritual search.

Free But Not Cheap

"The best things in life are free," the saying goes, and it is true of faith. But even though faith is free, it isn't cheap. Like love, it presents itself as a gift that you cannot buy, but rather must reject or receive ... and if you receive it, it costs you nothing—except the status quo. That's a price some people will not pay. How about you?

"But if faith costs me the status quo, if faith requires me to be open to change, what will I gain in return?" you ask. A fair question, but a hard one to answer ... at least, a hard one for one person to answer on paper or in words. The best way to find an answer is to observe the gains that have come to other people because of their faith. No, that's the second best way. The best way is to experiment yourself.

Gains

If you experiment with faith, if you observe the impact of faith on the lives of others, you will find that the flip side of each cost represents a beautiful gain. Let's consider our previous six examples:

1. *Humility (Pride)*. In spite of how little I know about humility, I do know this about pride: pride is tiring, a cruel taskmaster, a complicator, a destroyer. Humility, in contrast, relaxes, refreshes, relieves, simplifies, renews. To the degree that becom-

ing childlike includes becoming humble, humility releases child-like play, laughter, sleep, smiles, fun. Our pride forces us to take ourselves so seriously, which leads us to take others less seriously and God less seriously still. Humility prompts the reverse (note the etymological link between "humility" and "humus" and "humor" and "human"), bringing us down to earth (humus) and letting us have a good laugh at ourselves (humor) for who we are (human). Everything depends on you when you're proud; you're indispensable. That brings a lot of pressure. When you are childlike, humble, down-to-earth, small ... the pressure is gone. Losing pride is like going to the dentist with a root canal. It's scary and it hurts. But it feels so much better when the damned thing (I mean that literally, not as a vulgarity) is out!

2. *Community (Judgmentalism)*. If I have been worshiping at the altar of pride, it is rather hard to convince others to kneel down with me for very long. They have their own idols to worship, and besides, mine doesn't look all that good to them anyway. Remove that obstacle, and two things happen. First, I can simply enjoy other people without judging them, which tends to attract them a bit more than before. Second, I find a new and special kinship with other people of good faith, a kindred spirit often called "fellowship." This fellowship, when grounded on good faith (as opposed to other kinds of faith), creates an inclusive community spirit, breaks down barriers, and brings people together.

3. *Virtue (Vices)*. There's an old story about a preacher who was interrupted one day by a heckler. "I challenge you to a debate on God versus atheism," he shouted. The preacher responded, "I'll gladly have such a debate, under these conditions. You bring two people whose lives have been transformed by their belief in

atheism, and I'll bring two people whose lives have been transformed by their belief in God. This way, our debate can explore not only the content of our beliefs, but also the effects of our beliefs." The heckler declined the offer. The story illustrates the fact that wherever you find faith — from an AA meeting to a youth group, from an inner-city storefront church to a remote monastery, you will find people struggling (with God's help) for self-mastery, striving (with God's help) to become better people, aspiring (with God's help) to be freer of vice and fuller of virtue. Was it Martin Luther King Jr. who said, "I am not the man I would be, or the man I should be, but thank God Almighty, neither am I the man I once was!"?

4. *Balance (Imbalance)*. Faith gives life a center point around which to balance life's competing demands, opportunities, enjoyments. Faith gives life a reference point around which to proportion life's components. Faith gives life a reason to be lived gracefully and well.

5. *Passion (Apathy)*. It's sad — the image of the anemic, callow, thin-skinned, atrophied, weakling, insipid, petty, inconsequential, pathetic saint persists. How different from the vibrant reality of a tough and resilient Mother Teresa, a steady and bold Billy Graham, a wild and crazy youth group leader, a daring and innovative mission leader. Speaking personally, nothing could have made me work as long, hard, consistently, and sincerely as faith has these last twenty or so years — not money, not guilt, not pressure, not fame — only faith. Good faith launches more volunteerism, nurtures more love and neighborliness, inspires more social action, impassions more social justice, engenders more personal growth, and fires more virile visions than any other force on earth. The world is still in too short supply of these assets, you say? Yes — a fact which calls for more good faith!

6. *Generosity (Greed)*. There is something in life so much better than getting: giving. The joys of generosity exceed the joys of consumption and greed in both quantity and quality, not to mention intensity and persistence. Good faith always flowers into generosity in its many forms ... hospitality (generosity with my home), patience (generosity with my time), liberality (generosity with my funds), empathy (generosity with my emotions). Perhaps you have heard the play on the old question: "What do you give to the person who has everything?" Answer: generosity!

Again, as with the costs, these six gains are representative of a much longer list we could create. But any list of this sort, in a big way, misses the point. There is another gain, so obvious it's almost embarrassing to mention. Through faith (good faith, that is), you gain God.

Lunch with Karl

I had lunch the other day with a fascinating fellow. Karl was a pastor for many years, very successful by all normal standards. But during his second pastorate, he lost something—energy, hope, perspective, maybe even faith. Exhausted, burned out, sick and tired, he left the ministry. (This kind of story is far more common than you might think.)

What does a washed-up pastor do with his life—especially one with a family to support, a mortgage to pay, college tuition to anticipate? He got a job in finance, and worked his way up the ladder in a large investment firm. He hated the work, but he needed money. Eventually, he was hired on in a large retirement facility, and a year later his well-developed people skills won him attention as a candidate for the job of executive director—a position not unlike being the mayor of a town of several thousand senior citizens. A pretty good-sized "congregation"—with better-than-pastors' pay too, no doubt.

We had a really enjoyable lunch together. He looks very happy; he clearly loves his work, and is good at it. The whole place reflects his positive, upbeat attitude—residents and staff alike. (I was treated with extraordinary courtesy by everyone from the guard at the front gate to the waitress in one of the many cafeterias!)

Eleven Years Later

During the meal, we shared our stories. As the waitress cleared our dishes, our conversation went a level deeper. "When I left the ministry, my faith was devastated," he said. "Now, eleven years later, I cringe when I think back on many of my sermons. They were so abstract, so disconnected from real life. It was like I was in this little box, and things that seemed so important in that box seem so insignificant in the big world out here.

"I have a lot of questions now. There are a lot of things I was sure about back then, but now, I just don't know. Maybe some of it is midlife; maybe some of it is cynicism; maybe some of it is wisdom." After a pause, he continued, "But there was one sermon I preached at the very end, when I was so burned out. I could preach that sermon still today, because in spite of everything I've been through, I still know that sermon is true."

I asked him the title of the sermon. It came from a passage in the Old Testament: "I am my beloved's, and he is mine." The sermon had two parts, he said. Part 1: I am my beloved's. I belong to God. I am in God's care. I am one of God's children. Part 2: God is mine. God has given himself to me. He has entered my life, entered into relationship with me, connected with me. God is mine.

And that says it better than anything else could: What is the ultimate benefit of faith? Being able to know and feel what Karl knows and feels ... that no matter what, I am God's, and God is mine ... that we have a connection; we have a relationship. Faith in your life brings God in your life.

The Candle May Flicker, But It Won't Flicker Out

I know the search is hard at times. I know the candle of faith flickers. For reasons we have considered, and others as well, it is tempting indeed and all too easy to let the candle flicker out. I wonder how I can encourage you—knowing full well that I can't pressure you—not to let that happen. Perhaps sharing some more of my personal story is the best thing I can do. That's what the remaining chapters will offer.

Your Response

1. What costs do I anticipate in pursuing faith? Which have I already experienced?
2. What gains or benefits do I anticipate in pursuing faith? Which have I already experienced?
3. Under what circumstances might I be tempted to abort my search, and how might I avoid aborting my search?

Resources

Many people have been helped by embarking on a thirty-day experiment of faith. The idea is simple: for one month, you attempt to live as if God were real, even if you are not yet convinced of that. Each day, for these thirty days, you attempt to live what we could call the "Four G's":

A. Golden Rule: You try to "do unto others as you would have them do to you."
B. Gratitude: You try to thank God for every blessing you can, beginning with life, shelter, food, safety, health ... down to minute by minute pleasures and experiences.
C. Generosity: You try to give to others — time, hospitality, money, empathy, respect. You live with liberality, not miserliness.
D. Going: You determine to attend religious services for this month — to go faithfully.

You also might find it helpful to make prayer and Bible reading a daily habit during this time. Reading (or rereading) this book or reading some of the books recommended at the back of this book could enrich this time as well. If your findings are inconclusive after thirty days, sign on for another thirty.

Prayer

God, I must admit a certain ambivalence I have about you. While part of me is drawn to you, part of me is afraid of you or even resentful of you. I feel you pose a certain threat to me — at the very least, to my ego (since with you around, I am no longer Number One), and more practically, to my behavior (I am becoming aware of many shabby features of my life that need changing). I find that I need humility and courage as well as faith to continue this search, and I ask you for the humility to admit my needs and my faults, and the courage to be willing to change. I believe the changes you have in store for me will be for the best, but I find it hard to let go. I want to surrender my often stubborn will to you, God. Help me to do this even now. I believe that what I gain will be so much greater than what I lose. I want to let go of all I must let go of in order to have empty hands to receive all you want to give me. I believe that you love me. And one more thing: I am sorry for the many wrongs I have done. I would like to come clean with you about them whenever they arise, and rather than justify myself or make excuses or blame others, I would like to freely admit my wrongs and ask for your forgiveness and power to change.

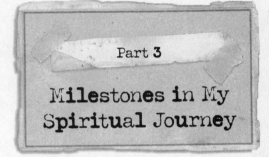

Part 3

Milestones in My
Spiritual Journey

Tadpoles on the Kitchen Table

This chapter attempts to convey my delight in finding God in creation.

Who Should Read This Chapter?

This chapter will be of special interest to nature lovers like myself, as well as those who feel that science and faith are enemies.

What Questions Does It Address?

How can nature be seen to reflect God? How does a faith approach to nature differ from a strictly scientific approach?

Just as science has found the power of the sun itself to be locked in the atom, so religion proclaims the glory of the eternal to be reflected in the simplest of elements of time: a leaf, a door, an unturned stone.

Huston Smith, *Beyond the Post-Modern Mind*

Tadpoles on the Kitchen Table

Here is what I remember about Olean, New York, where I was born. We had a big backyard—big in the eyes of a little boy, anyway (have you ever noticed how everything about your childhood home shrinks when you return as an adult?)—where you could find toads and leopard frogs. We had a rock garden where you could catch garter snakes and red-bellied snakes under the flat slate. We had a little brook next to the driveway, where the rocks had fossils in them, and under the rocks you could find crayfish and dusky salamanders. And across the dirt road there was a field with an electric fence (scary!) that was full of big cows, and sometimes you could see deer and maybe even a red fox in the early morning mist.

If you walked up the hill behind our house, you would come to Eiser's Pond—owned, no doubt, by the Eisers, whom I never actually met. I remember my dad taking me up there on a spring day. Frogs! Big ones! Jumping with a squeal or grunt into the water from the bank! And there, in the cattails, little black dots, perfect, in the clearest jelly, a mass, floating like a cloud of bold periods. Dad had boots on, and he waded in, scooped down with the plastic bucket, and came up with the frogs' eggs.

Back home, we put them in a goldfish bowl and put the goldfish bowl in the center of our kitchen table. (My parents loved my brother and me, indulging our boyhood interests to heroic degrees, as you can see.) Days passed in the mysterious way they do for children, not slow, not fast; they just passed. The little black periods turned into commas, and after some days, the commas wiggled! Soon the jelly melted away, and the little tadpoles became free swimming, and Dad must have put lettuce in the water, something to feed the little guys, because they grew.

At breakfast, I would ask, "How are they doing?" At lunch: "Are those little legs I see forming?" At dinner: "How much longer until they're frogs?" Thus began my love for nature, a love that still grows today.

Wrong Word

I am uncomfortable with the word "nature" in the last sentence, because I actually believe it would be truer to say, "Thus began my love for God." "Nature" feels like too autonomous a term, too much of a stand-alone, too disconnected from the Creator. Even as a boy, in every metamorphosing tadpole, every deer standing ears-erect in the mist, every white pine tree hiding a perfect robin's nest in a niche among its branches, every red-winged blackbird calling from a cattail, I could sense a taste of something so fine, something more, a precious treasure, a subtle clue, an enticing scent, a delicious hook. Now, though not then, of course, I see these as signs pointing to God. When I would lift a fossil-pocked rock in the creek bed by my house, uncovering a crayfish who would invariably wave its pincers defensively (like the old robot in Lost in Space—"Danger! Danger!"), its bulbous eyes finding me, its antennae held back like tiny horsewhips, I wasn't just seeing a "thing," a crustacean with some Latin name, I was seeing a piece of God's handiwork. A little funny, a little scary, but (in the words of a boy) "totally cool," its very coolness part of God's signature.

Imagine being five and crouching with me beside the cinder block foundation of my house. I would pull the grass back from the gray blocks, barely breathing, concentrating ... a gray pill bug, a black field cricket, a tiny brown toad, a striped baby garter snake, a red eft. A red eft! Have you ever seen one? What could be more beautiful than the delicate brick-orange back, the lighter yellowish underside lightly peppered with black dots, highlighted along the spine with two neat rows of red dots, each ringed in black. Such a beautiful creature, and so harmless. If you traveled thirty light-years to a distant solar system and emerged from your spacecraft to find delicate, colorful, benign creatures like this, you would travel home and tell your friends that the trip was worth it just to see such an amazing life-form! And here it is in my own backyard.

Who can assign a value to these creatures? Who can deny the existence of a Creator when viewing such wonders? Who can help but love these creatures, and in loving them, who can doubt that his or her love wants to reach through and beyond the creatures to their Creator?

A Song from College Years

Long before I began writing prose, I wrote songs, and many of my old song lyrics express my wonder and love for God-in-creation better than I now can in prose. This one was written while I was in college:

Your Majesty

I love to see your high white clouds sailing, Lord,
like a fleet of mighty galleons on the blue,
and watch white seagulls dive and glide among them.

Your Majesty, they make me think of you....
The rhythm and the roar of ocean breakers,
    like great dark pages they turned as the tide
    withdrew.
They curled and they crashed and they pounded the surf
    in the white foam.
    Your Majesty, they make me think of you....
I love to watch the dark gray clouds as a storm's
    approaching,
    and see the willow branches sway as the wind blows
    through...
see the flash of lightning, hear the rumbling of your
    thunder.
    Your Majesty, they make me think of you....
Upon a tall and mighty mountain, with a valley spread
    below (so beautiful)
    I lean into a strong fast breeze and deep inside I
    know,
that all of creation joins in majestic declaration, from a
    single leaf and flower of clover to a burning yellow
    star to show,
    Your Majesty, how wonderful you are!
Your salmon spawn after fighting up fast river currents.
    Your geese migrate each season as you taught them to.
Your great sea turtles return to the beach of their birth.
    Your Majesty, they make me think of you....

Years later, this song expressed a similar sentiment:

The Glory of God

There's a farm that I know, as a child I would go, and
    run in its fields below.

Near a barn on a hill stood an old windmill, and in the
afternoon sun it would glow
… with the glory of God, the glory of God, the glory of
God shining through.
And I pray for you that you will see it too, for this life is a
search for the glory of God….
There are people I've met whom I'll never forget, full of
laughter, some young and some old.
Sometimes on a face, this mysterious grace seems to smile
out and shine out like gold.
It's the glory of God, the glory of God, the glory of God
shining through.
And I pray for you that you will see it too, for this life is a
search for the glory of God….
There are moments that come like a gift from someone
who loves you, but you hardly know.
They bring a tear to the cheek, and a catch when you
speak, and the meaning you seek seems to flow…
with the glory of God, the glory of God, the glory of God
shining through.
And I pray for you that you will see it too, for this life is a
search for the glory of God….

Nothing Buttery

Everyone who knew me as a boy was certain that I would
grow up to be a scientist of some sort, given my love for all things
natural. I remember in eighth grade, looking forward so much
to taking biology—a chance during school hours to indulge a
personal delight—for fun and credit! But I also remember a
huge disappointment as I realized that science studied animals

in every way except the way that counted most to me: simply as living beings, full of fascination and wonder. It renamed creatures as organisms, dissected organisms into systems, and reduced systems to chemistry, chemistry to physics, physics to mathematics. I have heard this reduction process called "nothing but-tery." That red eft? That's nothing but a larval stage of the primitive vertebrate amphibian *notophthalmus viridescens*. That sunset? That's nothing but light being refracted through humid atmosphere. That house finch singing? That's nothing but a territorial organism's way of marking territory using sound: some other organisms use the smell of urine for the same purpose.

Eighth-Grade Biology

Eighth-grade biology taught me that I would rather pursue my interest in the natural world on my own, having been thoroughly turned off by scientific reductionism, where everything is "understood" when it has finally been reduced to a numeric equation or a Latin name of some sort. It is amazing that any sense of wonder survives that kind of education. It strikes me now, looking back, as a kind of sick brainwashing, a kind of secular fundamentalism that is too proud, rigid, and closed-minded to admit a sense of awe, to acknowledge the mystery beyond the rim of mathematical orthodoxy. I guess that is why I decided to pursue literature and music instead of science; they allowed me to explore and celebrate the very things that science seemed determined to explain away as "nothing but ..."

I think things have changed a bit even since my childhood. I sense that secular scientific fundamentalism is softening. Just the other day, while reading an article about spirituality in a local publication called *The Washingtonian*, I came across a new term. Our postmodern world was referred to as a "postsecular world," and I thought, "Yes, how fitting. Secularism is running out of steam. people are finally coming to realize the bankruptcy of an approach to life that claims to explain everything by little equations." The poet William Wordsworth complained in the early 1800s about the scientific approach that would "murder to dissect"—and nearly two hundred years later, the rest of us are finally seeing some wisdom in Wordsworth's indictment.

Doubting Secular Fundamentalism

Let's pause here a little longer. Think about your scientific education. It was based on an unspoken, hardly recognized assumption—a dogmatic tenet of secular faith, really: that everything is completely explainable by our going back and understanding its causes or by tearing it apart and understanding its parts, as if the parts were the cause of the whole. Cause-effect thus becomes the key to everything. As you read these words, you might say, "Of course. What else is there?" That reaction, I think you will see, proves how well we have been taught a certain secular orthodoxy ... an orthodoxy that is crumbling as we progress to a postsecular world.

Now you might expect me to say, "But if we trace all cause-effect chains back far enough, back billions of years, we come to the Big Bang, and since that cause itself can't be explained within a closed system of cause and effect, there must be a God." I could say that, and I actually do believe that, but that's not my point here at all. Rather, I want to help you see something much bigger, something I have only come to see in recent months and have never tried to articulate until today.

There is another way—an equally valid perspective—to try to understand things, a way that is not opposed to the cause-effect approach but rather encompasses it and enriches it, a way that in fact reinjects the sense of wonder and awe into the secular nothing-buttery approach by cracking it open to new light and fresh air. We could call it the purpose approach. Cause-effect looks back and asks, "What caused this?" Purpose looks up or ahead, and asks, "And why was it caused? For what purpose? For what end?" Cause-effect looks for a force pushing events from behind. Purpose looks for a pattern or design or intention or meaning pulling events from ahead, guiding them from above, enriching them from within.

Seeing the Absurdities

My secular education taught me—never directly, of course, and perhaps all the more convincingly because of its subtlety —that any approach other than cause-effect was superstitious, primitive, backward. It never proved that assertion; its only argument was to ignore questions of purpose, or if they arose, to scoff at them, call them belittling names. Hardly a scientific approach! The rejection of purpose in a tight, closed, cause-effect system is, upon further investigation, at least ironic and at most downright absurd. There is certainly no logical requirement to so limit our inquiry. Here is how I summarized the absurdity in my previous book:

> ... Freudianism says that all beliefs and behaviors flow out of certain psychosexual complexes ... all beliefs except, of course, Freudianism, and all behaviors except, of course, the behavior of expounding Freudianism.

Evolutionism says that all characteristics, including the development of thinking brains, are selected naturally to favor survival ... not necessarily the apprehension of truth; this belief suggests that the very organ which conceives of evolution is oriented to produce useful theories, but not necessarily true ones. Marxism and Skinnerian behaviorism alike suggest that individual human behaviors are determined ... whether by class-struggle or pain-avoidance mechanisms ... conveniently excluding the behaviors of the theorists themselves, who speak and write as if their theories were generated in the vacuum of a pure search for truth rather than in the mechanism of their own socio-economic or intrapersonal dynamics. And radical [pluralism] rejects the universal truthfulness of every other belief while assuming its own position as the only universally true one. (*The Church on the Other Side*, Grand Rapids: Zondervan, 2000, pp. 171–72)

The very people who claim to have explained everything by their cause-effect system can't explain themselves or their own quest for truth—which is an act of purpose, not merely of cause and effect.

Eyeglasses

In many ways, we are like farsighted people who are understandably and legitimately thrilled by how much more detail we now see because of our new eyeglasses (secular science) than we ever saw before without them. The problem comes when our being thrilled with our new clarity of vision leads to being overly impressed with ourselves, our progressiveness, our advancement, our technology, our great vision — so impressed, that we become unwilling to have our vision examined again. We have become unwilling to accept the possibility that our current prescription — given to us by the modern, secular, scientific world — has blinded us to some big things even as it helped us see other littler ones, distorted and blurred things at some distances even as it sharpened things at others, made some things disappear even as it brought others into focus.

Now, as we enter the postsecular age, perhaps we will be able to see that as wonderful as our scientific education has been, it's time to drop its rigid, fundamentalistic dogmatism and open our eyes again to see the parts of life that can't be fully explained by cause-effect (though they certainly can partially be so explained). Then, the wonder will begin to return, as we recognize that purpose, design, meaning, and pattern have a place after all. This new vision is the finding of faith.

Obviously, as a boy, I had no language to articulate this kind of discomfort with the predominant worldview I was being educated in. In fact, I was caught in a double bind. My religious world gave me one version of fundamentalism that refused to be open to the insights of science, while my secular world gave me this scientific fundamentalism unwilling to see anything brought to the table by faith. In other words, science forbade me to see anything in the universe other than nails, equipped as it was with this one hammer of cause and effect. But I do remember a kind of enlightening moment that came during my college years — almost silly in its simplicity, but perhaps you will be able to relate, because you have probably had similar experiences.

The Entomological Argument

I remember doing homework at a picnic table when a tiny bug landed on my shirtsleeve. It walked this way, then that. It reached up its front legs and took hold of its left antenna, bent it down, and washed it in its mouthparts. Then it walked around a bit more, then repeated the washing procedure with the right antenna, and then flew away. An inconsequential event. But I remember thinking, "That tiny bug. Why did it decide to land here, walk there, and wash its antennae now, not later? It's not enough to tell me about its evolutionary development or its biological drives for food, comfort, and reproduction. No, this little creature really is alive! It really makes choices! It's not just a mathematical equation, a totally determined organism in an environment. It really is alive and lives with its own purposes!"

And the train of thought continued: If alive and purposeful, then there is something in the universe called life and purpose, and if life and purpose, then there must be a source of life and purpose. Aquinas and Anselm (great theologians who posited powerful intellectual arguments for the existence of God) must make room for this newest proof—the Entomological Argument for the Existence of God—"If there are living, purposeful bugs, there must be a God." The wonder returns!

The Old Box Is Too Small

That wonder has been for me through the years an increasingly powerful apologetic (an argument for the existence of God). I know that some folk out there can attempt to "nothing-butterize" the sense of wonder itself, but I also know that I would be denying my truest sense of how things really are to go along with them. I can't squeeze everything back into the cause-effect box anymore. Purpose, and along with it design and pattern and meaning, won't fit its narrow confines. It's not enough to feel smug about naming elements in a cause-effect chain — especially if the chain itself is part of something bigger, something with pattern, meaning, design, and purpose.

As I said before, evolution doesn't bother me. If you tell me that God created the earth "by hand" in six days some thousands of years ago, I am impressed. If you tell me instead that God set a whole cosmos in motion some billions of years ago, a cosmos perfectly calibrated within the narrowest of margins to produce at least one planet where life would be developed through cause-effect chains that were designed into it by a purposeful Designer ... I am no less impressed; in fact, I may be even more impressed. The "how" and "when" of it all seem almost inconsequential to me compared to the "what" and "why" which lie beyond cause and effect.

Unchanging

I am in my fifties now, but you will still find me crouching down to see a red eft hiding in the moss, whenever I get the chance. Whenever I can, I head up to a stretch of the Potomac River a couple of hours from here, for a five-mile walk that I have taken in various seasons, under varying weather conditions, over many years now. The mountains change as the seasons change, from grays and browns to palest greens, to bold emeralds to bright crimsons and blazing yellows, to fading ambers and darkening rusts.... The river changes through floods and droughts, sometimes opaque butterscotch brown, sometimes so clear you can see the wood turtles scrambling and bounding along the rocky bottom like astronauts on the moon.

The vegetation changes, the birdsongs change, the insects change, and everything changes, everything but this: As the psalmist said, "The heavens declare the glory of God; the skies proclaim the work of his hands." To me in my fifties no less than at five, the world rings like a struck bell with this resonance: There is a God, and God is alive, and God is good, and God is beautiful. There is cause and effect explorable by science, but the very chains of cause and effect are linked in a purpose and pattern and meaning that goes beyond anything secular orthodoxy can explain. I guess you could say that in my experience, science keeps leading me to faith, ever since tadpoles wiggled like lively commas on my kitchen table in Olean, New York.

Your Response

1. In what ways does nature/creation enrich your faith?
2. Where can I go in the coming week or month to enjoy some facet of creation, and in so doing, enjoy the Creator?

Resources

Annie Dillard's *Pilgrim at Tinker Creek* offers musings on creation that are enriching to one's faith. And, of course, there are many excellent nature guides to help you learn to appreciate the rich endowment of species of plant and animal life that surround us.

Prayer

God, I thank you and honor you for your artistry in creation. It is truly amazing and awe-inspiring. In particular, I want to thank you for ... (Complete this prayer with your own thoughts.)

Jesus Anonymous

This chapter explores the role of Jesus in the spiritual search, acknowledging the sad failure of Christians to represent him very well.

Who Should Read This Chapter?

People who are unsure what to make of Jesus.

What Questions Does It Address?

Why are some people turned off by the word "Jesus"? Are there reasons to push beyond these turnoffs?

After a sampling of ten negative images many people associate with Jesus, the chapter explores some more positive and hopeful associations.

Jesus of Nazareth has been the dominant figure in the history of Western culture for almost twenty centuries. If it were possible, with some sort of super magnet, to pull up out of that history every scrap of metal bearing at least a trace of his name, how much would be left?

Jaroslav Pelikan, *Jesus through the Centuries*

For they concur with the thought John Donne put poetically in his sonnet on the Resurrection, where he says of Christ,

> *He was all gold when He lay down, but rose*
> *All tincture....*

Donne was referring to the alchemists, whose ultimate hope was to discover not a way of making gold but a tincture that would transmute into gold all the baser metals it touched. A Christian is someone who has found no tincture equal to Christ.

Huston Smith, *The World's Religions*

Jesus Anonymous

No one has had a greater influence on my life than Jesus. But I have to confess: I have a love-hate relationship with "Jesus." I mean, of course, the name, the word—not the person. To be sure, I keep growing in love for the person behind the name. But the name makes me squirm sometimes.

Maybe you feel the same way. It is hard, here, at the beginning of the twenty-first century, to say or hear the name "Jesus" without thinking of some or all of the following:

1. A big-haired lady caked with too much makeup, or a toupeed man whose face moves way too much when he talks, staring DIRECTLY into your eyes through the television screen, with an intensity so overdone as to defy all interpretations of honesty or sincerity, entreating you to believe in Jesus. They are telling you, yelling at you, that they see—RIGHT NOW! AT THIS MOMENT!—a tumor of exactly the kind you have recently been diagnosed with—being COMPLETELY HEALED in the name of JESUS! (Never mind that the show was prerecorded, so that "right now" has little meaning. Also never mind that your tumor is not healed, or that even if it is, thousands of others aren't.)

2. "Jesus saves" graffiti, common from highway abutments in Philadelphia to roadside signs posted on

trees in Georgia to bumper stickers seen at all points south and west. What exactly the graffiti is supposed to communicate remains unclear ... and why anyone would think that vandalism-evangelism would be more helpful than hurtful to travelers who read it is anybody's guess.

3. Overlong, boring church services, where things like "Jesus is God" or "Jesus is Lord" or "Son of God" are said so often and with such familiarity that it seems inappropriate to ask what they mean ... even though you realize that you have next to no idea. If you do ask, it becomes embarrassingly apparent that the person whom you are asking has never been asked this question before, or, if he has, still hasn't figured out an answer that you can understand.

4. Any one of many movies about Jesus in which he nearly always (choose any three of the following): (a) speaks with a British accent; (b) has unquestionably Anglo-Saxon (and therefore non-Semitic) features, including but not limited to wavy brown hair, creamy white skin, and/or dreamy blue eyes; (c) pauses a little bit too long between ... sentences and ... phrases as ... if ... to ... suggest ... that he is really tuned in ... to another frequency than ... the ... rest ... of us; (d) walks "floatingly," as if he just got off roller skates, or else has a bad back; (e) never seems to smile or laugh, and therefore hardly seems like the kind of person children or fishermen (not to mention wine-imbibers and prostitutes) would have enjoyed being around.

5. Various ongoing scholarly inquiries into "the historical Jesus," seeking to liberate Jesus from the straitjacket of myth and prejudice from the past. These projects have produced much of value, but unfortunately, too often immediately following his liberation from past myth and prejudice, he is then reinserted into the even more confining modern straitjacket of nineteenth- and twentieth-century myth and prejudice (just in time to be outdated for the twenty-first century).

6. The slogan "Jesus is the only way!" — which seems to you frightfully narrow-minded, exclusive, arrogant, and insulting. This slogan is repeated incessantly by many of Jesus' most ardent followers, and the more you question what is meant by it, the louder it is repeated back to you. (Granted, those who repeat the slogan most ardently intend it as neither frightful, narrow-minded, exclusive, arrogant, or insulting. It is, rather, a sincere way of saying that they really believe in him. More on that later.)

7. People who seem to show up at your door just as you are trying to leave (or sleep), or slide up beside you on an airplane just as you are trying to read (or sleep), or confront you on a sidewalk just as you are trying to get away from them, and ask, sometimes smiling but more often nervously, "Do you know Jesus personally?" or "Are you saved?" or "Are you born again?"

8. Some of the schmaltziest and weirdest music you have ever heard, played on seven out of eight radio stations in certain parts of the country, in between which preachers vary their pronunciation from "JAY-zuss" to "GEEzis."

9. A pink, well-fed baby featured in nativity scenes and on Christmas cards, almost always eliciting the cry, "Ahh, how cute"—probably the last words anyone would have actually said about the actual Jesus.

10. The holocaust, slavery, the rape of the environment during the Industrial Era, the subjugation or annihilation of native peoples and/or their cultures, oppression of women, opposition to free speech, politically inflammatory rhetoric (such as "We're gonna take back this country for JAYzuss!" etc., etc.), the bombing of abortion clinics, the reckless calling down of damnation on anyone and everyone, witch hunts, inquisitions, suppression of scientific inquiry, and any one of a dozen other horrors done or defended by somebody somewhere in the name of you-know-who.

If It Weren't for the Christians

It pains me to write these things. But twenty centuries of Christianity have led many people (including Friedrich Nietzsche) to say, "It would be a whole lot easier to believe in Christ if it weren't for the Christians."

If Jesus were to reappear among us today, I wouldn't be surprised if he would call himself Mike or Sue or Abdul or Nikita or George or Carol. Or more likely, he might remain completely anonymous—anything to distance himself from the image believers like me too often create for him. We Christians have, I am brokenhearted to admit, succeeded after twenty centuries at turning the name "Jesus" into an obscenity for many people in many places around the world.

A Third-Millennial Birthday Gift

I say "we Christians" because I too am part of the problem, far too often. I often think that one of the greatest gifts we Christians could give to Jesus at the two-thousandth anniversary of his adult ministry would be to just shut up about him for a few years, during which time we would try to come to terms with what a mess we have made of the simple path that he introduced to planet earth (and which we quickly complicated, confused, and corrupted), during which time we would simply try to practice what he preached, especially the parts about loving God and loving our neighbors, during which time we would stop producing Jesus-junk (pencils, T-shirts, screen savers, bumper stickers, plastic mugs, refrigerator magnets, and the like, with his name embossed upon them, which successfully merchandise and therefore cheapen his name) and try to rediscover some sense of reverence, dignity, and good taste.

After a few years of that, perhaps we could say his name again on rare occasions and it wouldn't sound so frivolous, so stained, so obscene. And perhaps we wouldn't then embarrass him so much. (Having said that, I realize he must have a level of security, virtue, and maturity that put him far beyond embarrassment ... qualities I evidently lack, since I can't understand how he puts up with our shenanigans.)

I Can't Be Serious

Let me indulge this fantasy a little more. I am a preacher. Maybe for the next twenty-five years, no sermon preached by my colleagues and me should be permitted to go beyond four minutes in length, as a way of admitting that we know next to nothing of Jesus, so we should say next to nothing for a change.

Maybe we should declare a twenty-five-year moratorium on all baptisms; after all, since we seem to have forgotten what being a Christian is all about, how can we induct others onto the path with any confidence? Maybe apologetics (the reasoned defense of one's faith) should actually spend the next twenty-five years apologizing—for all the things thoughtlessly, roughly, stupidly done with either misguided zeal or unguided apathy. Maybe the Billy Graham of the twenty-first century should reverse the method of Jesus, and not call sinners to repentance, but rather should call religious people to repentance, since they have become the best excuse for sinners to keep sinning and for the cynics to remain jaded. Obviously, I can't be serious. Or can I?

Serious or not, I can't finish this book on finding faith without telling you, as sincerely as I can, what a crucial role this unnamed person has had in the finding and formation of my faith. But as you can see, this is awkward for me ... not because I am ashamed of the real Jesus, but because I am so ashamed of what we Christians have made of him to people like you. I have no authorization to do this, but I'll bet a million Christians would add their hearty amen if they heard me say this: I want to apologize to you, a person sincerely seeking faith, for the mess we Christians have made of Jesus and his whole enterprise. I am so sorry.

Thankfully, there are still a few stars sparkling in this dark sky. Let me tell you about one of these brighter examples.

Sisavanh's Statement

For several years back in the eighties, I taught English as a second language to adult refugees and foreign students here in the U.S.—Cambodian, Vietnamese, Laotian, Chinese, Ethiopian,

Iranian, Afghan, and others. What wonderful memories I have of these splendid people! I remember one day, we were having a somewhat free-ranging discussion about the cultures represented in our class. One student, a Lao, talked about being Buddhist. Then, with characteristic respect, he asked me, "Teacher, what religion you?" (Obviously, I had not done too well yet teaching the verb "to be.")

"I am a Christian," I said. And this fellow—I believe Sisavanh was his name—said, "Oh, Teacher, we love all Christian. When I escape my country, the communist want to kill me, and I go to refugee camp in Thailand. I go there, and I don't know nobody. I have nothing, no money, no food, no family. But Christian people there, they give me everything. They give me food, clothing, medicine, blanket, place to stay. They teach me a little English. I never forget them for that. That why I love all Christian. Very good, very good."

Wonders

As Sisavanh spoke, so energized, so sincere, dozens of heads were nodding in agreement. At refugee camps around the world—in Thailand, Pakistan, Greece, the Philippines—these people had felt a touch of love that came through people motivated by Jesus Christ. That, I thought, must make Jesus proud. True, there are far too many embarrassments said and done in the name of Jesus. But there are also many wonders.

I don't know what you think of Jesus. I hope you have met at least a few people who impressed you as those missionaries in the refugee camps impressed my students. I hope the other kind of impressions—the bombastic, the insensitive, the disrespectful, the rude, the arrogantly narrow-minded—haven't completely alienated you. If you think about it (I hope I am not trying to make excuses here), the bad behavior of Christians tells you less about Christ than it does about human nature. After all, what other raw material does Christ have to work with? If he tried to exclude anyone who might embarrass him, whom would he be left with? (Certainly not me.) Perhaps we shouldn't be surprised that we flub things up so grandly.

Butterflies, Lightning, Wind, Spring

I don't want to make it sound like I have Jesus all figured out. I don't. Nearly every Sunday for many years I have preached about Jesus and his teachings. That means that every week I have pondered Jesus and his message for hours on end. I have read hundreds of books about Jesus and his message and his ongoing mission on earth, and I have done some writing myself. But still, I must confess that Jesus in many ways eludes me, even as he attracts me.

Behind the pages of the gospels — the four accounts of Jesus' life included in the New Testament — I find someone really there, someone substantial, too real, too vigorous, too alive, too robust to be reduced to a quick formula or set of principles. I push, and he pushes back. He won't be domesticated, mastered, outlined, packaged, shrink-wrapped, or nailed down (at least, not for long). That is frustrating at times. But it is also quite wonderful.

Dead or Alive?

After all, it's only the dead butterflies that you can put on pins and display in glass cases. Live ones require you to enjoy their beauty in quick, stolen glances, iridescent here on this clover, swaying there on that goldenrod, pausing over there for a few moments for a drink beside that puddle, soon up again dazzling and skipping along on the breeze. Similarly, lightning can't be captured in a bottle; the wind can't be conveyed via propositions; springtime can't be unleashed on demand. I have found Jesus to have the same elusive but blazing vibrancy and reality. This is why I have come to believe in God as I have, and why I believe in Jesus. You, of course, may disagree or remain unconvinced, and I certainly understand that. As I have said, we Christians on the whole haven't made it easy for you.

Your Response

1. What are your impressions and beliefs about Jesus?
2. Which aspects of Jesus' teaching do you agree with, or disagree with?
3. What people seem to you to reflect the spirit of Jesus?
4. What do you wish to learn about Jesus, and how might you do this?

Resources

Three modern books on the life of Jesus stand out in my opinion: *The Jesus I Never Knew* by Philip Yancey; *The Lord* by Romano Guardini, and *The Case for Christ* by Lee Strobel. A wonderful book on the teachings of Jesus is Dallas Willard's *The Divine Conspiracy*. Of course, even more important would be to begin reading one of the four gospels (short biographies of Jesus) on your own. Luke is probably the most accessible and rewarding for modern readers; Mark is the shortest; John is a bit more philosophical and actually focuses on the issue of faith; and Matthew shows the most connection with the Jewish roots of Jesus' teachings. To return to the theme of chapter 4, I would also recommend connecting with a Type 3 faith community to put your explorations into a relational context.

My book *The Secret Message of Jesus* should be helpful too.

Prayer

God, if Jesus is truly from you, I want to know it. If what he says about you is true, I want to understand it, believe it, and live it. If following Jesus is the best way for me to grow closer to you, that is what I want to do. Help me to get a true glimpse of Jesus. Reading this book has been a start for me, or a new step in my spiritual search. But I don't want to stall in my journey. I want to keep moving ahead. Guide me in the next steps I should take to continue to nurture this relationship with you. I hear stories of other people whose lives have been touched by you and transformed by their faith in you. God, I look forward to the unique relationship I will develop and experience with you. Give me a faith that is not only good for me, but is also a positive example for others who need faith.

On a Maryland Hillside

This chapter recounts a very personal story of a pivotal experience of God in my life. It begins with some additional reflections on Jesus, continued from the previous chapter.

Who Should Read This Chapter?

This chapter will be of interest to anyone pursuing a spiritual quest.

What Questions Does It Address?

What experiences caused this author to pursue a spiritual search?

... when we came over the rise where the sea and land opened up to us, I stood in stunned silence and then slowly walked toward the waves. Words cannot capture the view that confronted me. I saw space and light and texture and color and power ... that seemed hardly of this earth. Gradually there crept into my mind the realization that God sees this all the time. He sees it, experiences it, knows it from every possible point of view, this and billions of other scenes like and unlike it, in this and billions of other worlds. Great tidal waves of joy must constantly wash through his being. It is perhaps strange to say, but suddenly I was extremely happy for God and thought I had some sense of what an infinitely joyous consciousness he is and of what it might have meant for him to look at his creation and find it "very good." ... he is simply one great inexhaustible and eternal experience of all that is good and true and beautiful and right. This is what we must think of when we hear theologians and philosophers speak of him as a perfect being. This is his life.

Dallas Willard, *The Divine Conspiracy*

On a Maryland Hillside

The words of Dallas Willard preceding this chapter ring true with me with a rare intensity. I remember sitting at my desk a few years ago, and a simple thought hit me out of the blue with similar intensity. It came in the form of a question: Is it possible to have a thought of God that is too good to be true? A God as wonderful as Willard described—a God of whom no thought can be too good—that is the God I have become convinced of and the God I have been seeking all my life.

That is why the teachings, story, and spirit of Jesus Christ have been so catalytic in my own spiritual journey. His life rings with this kind of vision of God. If I could somehow rescue Jesus from our miserable PR job (not that he really needs my help) and present him to people seeking faith, here are five things I would try to convey. (You will notice that these observations have little to do with the doctrines of the Trinity, incarnation, atonement, or the like. That's not because these doctrines aren't important, but rather because this is a book on finding faith, not furnishing it or fine-tuning it.)

1. Jesus Is Intellectually Honest

If there was one thing Jesus was clearly against, it was hypocrisy, pretense, cover-up, dishonesty. He wouldn't want you to recite a creed you were not convinced of. He wouldn't want you to pretend. He would rather have you say, "Lord, I believe, but yet I don't believe at the same time. I have my doubts, but I would like to work them through. Help me."

One of the most fascinating phrases to come frequently from Jesus' lips was this: "Believe because." That's why those who attempt to be faithful to Jesus and to show their complete allegiance to Jesus by saying, "Jesus is the only way! Jesus is the only way!" can be wrong even if they are right. In other words, even if Jesus is the only way, exactly as they understand him to be, Jesus himself wouldn't go around claiming that for himself without providing evidence; he wouldn't demand people to believe that without giving them good reason. Can you imagine Jesus saying, "Believe that I am the only way. Why? Because I said so, that's why! And if you don't believe, then you're going straight to hell!" But isn't that how we present him through our slogans?

No, again and again we find Jesus saying, not "Believe because I said so!" but rather "Believe because of the quality of my teachings. Believe because you see the miracles I do. Believe because you see my disciples love one another. Believe because you see my followers displaying a mysterious but real unity. Believe because my words prove true in experience. Believe because you can see my profile in the writings of the ancient prophets. Believe because God somehow makes it clear to you. Believe because credible people tell you that they saw me alive after being killed. Believe because the fruit of my life was good."

In other words, the faith that Jesus calls for is an intellectually honest faith, not a phony, forced, or inflated faith. If you see things that seem unjust or that just don't make sense—like religious people giving all their money to the church, while neglecting their elderly parents, or like pastors working hard to make converts who then become more miserable and unfree than they were before, or like churches being fastidious about minor matters (like rigorously avoiding labor on the Sabbath) while overlooking major matters (like loving their wives, treating their children gently, or loving their neighbors of other races) — if you see these kinds of things, you don't have to pretend they are okay. You can be honest. You can call a spade a spade; dirt, dirt; and manure, manure. He won't chide you for telling the truth. If you read the accounts of his life, this complete, transparent honesty comes through.

For example, one of his chosen twelve, Thomas, was a doubter, and of him Jesus didn't say, "Boy, did I make a mistake choosing you. I want believers around here, not skeptics!" No, instead he said, "Blessed are you, Thomas, because you demanded evidence. And after you received sufficient evidence, you were truly open-minded, so you believed." In other words, "Thomas, you had your honest doubts, but then when the evidence came through, you were honest enough to believe. I applaud you for that."

If Jesus is right, then God doesn't want a faith that is false, forced, make-believe, faked; he wants a faith that is honest — full of doubt and hope, questioning and risking, tentative exploration, gentle persuasion, and hard-won conviction. In my search for a faith that is real, I find that tremendously exhilarating!

2. Jesus Is Scandalously Inclusive

In the last chapter, when I seemed to knock those who say, "Jesus is the only way," some of you were thinking this: "But just a minute, Brian. Didn't Jesus' disciple John quote him as saying, 'I am the way and the truth and the life. No one comes to the Father except through me'" (John 14:6)? Isn't this "only way" language coming from Jesus' own mouth?

I would respond, "Yes. Absolutely. And I believe what Jesus said. But don't misconstrue that one statement; don't try to use it in a way Jesus himself never would use it." Because Jesus was not exclusive, at least not in the way the "Jesus is the only way" slogan makes him sound. Instead of Jesus being the way, the slogan makes it sound as if he is *in* the way—as if there are people trying to come to God and truth and life, but Jesus is blocking their path, keeping them out until they in some way acknowledge him. That's absurd. Rather, the reverse was true: Jesus was always the one helping in those whom others kept out! In the gospel narratives, we repeatedly see this theme of tension between exclusive followers (or disciples) and an inclusive Jesus.

For example, his disciples tried to exclude children, but Jesus said, "Let them come!" His disciples tried to exclude non-Jews, but Jesus said of one of them—a Roman centurion, no less!—"I have not found such great faith even in Israel!" His disciples tried to exclude people who were doing spiritual works in his name, but didn't travel in their circle, but Jesus said, "Whoever is not against us is for us."

My friend Neil Livingstone says it something like this: In a world of religious in-groups and out-groups, Jesus created a "come on in" group. The kingdom of God is open to everyone who will come, he said. It's like a party to which everyone is invited, rich or poor, employed or unemployed, clean or dirty. So scandalously inclusive was Jesus' teaching that it took decades before his top disciple, Peter, could really accept it (see Acts 10), and even then, Peter waffled in his endorsement of Jesus' come-on-in policy (see Galatians 2). It was just too radical.

Driving Conflict

Even more dramatic than the tension between Jesus and his disciples was the tension between Jesus and the most highly religious leaders of his day, known as the "Pharisees," perhaps meaning the "Separated Ones." In many ways, this tension is the driving conflict in the drama of Jesus' plotline.

Though it meant he earned the derisive label "friend of sinners," Jesus scandalized the Separated Ones by refusing to separate himself from prostitutes, tax collectors, lepers, rabble. The Separated Ones feared being contaminated by the sin of the sinful; Jesus, in contrast, knew that the intense power of his love could decontaminate the sinners by bringing them to repentance. In fact, he said, many of the last shall be first, and the first last, for precisely this reason: The Pharisees and the other highly religious people thought they saw it all. They thought they had arrived first at the destination of holiness and were in no need of repentance. They were good and holy—and proud of it, too. For that very reason, according to Jesus, they risked exclusion. Ironically, it wasn't the whores and crooks that Jesus threatened with hell. Read the gospels and you will find it was the religious who heard the rhetoric of fire and brimstone! The very opposite of our approach. Scandalous!

Here, then, the scandal worked in the opposite direction: The very people everyone considered most holy, most guaranteed of inclusion because of their immense knowledge of the Holy Scriptures and their rigor in obeying, were, according to Jesus, most in danger of exclusion. Perhaps you side with the Pharisees. That is certainly your choice. But I find Jesus' scandalous inclusion a powerful sign of his legitimacy. It rings true with me.

3. Jesus Is Relationally Electric

As you read the gospel accounts, watch him interact with Peter—now encouraging him, now confronting him, now encouraging him again, bringing him along so patiently, yet so relentlessly. With Peter as with all the disciples, Jesus has the toughness and tenderness of the best of coaches, determined to turn paunchy couch potatoes into star athletes with lean muscles and strong backbones and a will to win. It is a little scary, but I find myself wanting to sign on the team.

Or watch him interact with a nameless young leader, successful and bright, a sincere spiritual seeker. Watch him feel along the edges of this fellow's character to the one fault line that must be confronted: his love for money. Watch him challenge the man, not rushing him or pressuring him to change immediately, giving him time, letting him leave, regarding him with love even as he walks away.

Watch him with a woman, a multiple divorcée, a member of a despised minority group, chatting naturally as a friend, beside a well in Samaria, gently kindling her curiosity, teasing out her spiritual thirst as he discusses physical thirst. Watch him bring up the sensitive issue of her sexual relationship with men, and watch him do so in a way that she runs back to town and invites these men, along with everyone else who had no doubt whispered about her affairs, to come meet Jesus too. Amazing!

You might say, "But how do you know these stories are true? How do you know that someone didn't make them up?" Of course, I don't know. As we have seen in previous chapters, absolute certainty is not available on many, if any, things in this life for us. But I can say this: These stories are so improbable, so unexpected, so challenging to the status quo, so idiosyncratic, so earthy and rough and unedited and unrehearsed, that they simply seem to have the ring of truth to them, and so I believe them. And more, the truths that these stories yield are so inspiring that if they are fiction, whoever made them up would appear to deserve the honor we Christians give to Christ himself! But then again, if the stories are fraudulent, we are left with a paradox: It seems unlikely that a fraud—someone capable of perpetrating such a grand hoax—could ever come up with such spiritually inspiring fabrications. It seems unlikely that someone so sinister and dishonest could create stories of such simple genuineness and unpretentious grandeur.

Here is what strikes me after all these years of interacting with these stories: The electricity I sense as Jesus interacts with this amazing assortment of people, from prostitutes to Pharisees, from revolutionaries to military officers, resonates powerfully with the spiritual dynamic I sense in my own relationship with God. I sense this same electricity in my experience of life. Again, it rings true.

4. Jesus Is Graciously Demanding

Two kinds of religion are common in the world, it seems to me. First, there is no shortage of religion that is demanding—and graceless. Do this, don't eat that, travel here, say that, give this, accept that, observe this, forego that. And if you fail, you lose. Game over.

Second, and probably even more common these days, is gracious religion free of demand. You treat your wife like dirt? It's okay; after all, you weren't properly potty trained as a child. You broke your wedding vows? Nobody's perfect; it's okay. You make lots of money and keep it all to yourself? Not everybody is a Mother Teresa; it's okay. You drink too much, or listen too little, or complain excessively, or show gratitude infrequently or never? So do lots of other people, and we must maintain a good self-image, so it's okay.

Do you see the problem? Graceless demands leave us feeling guilty and defeated. Demandless grace leaves us apathetic and self-righteous. What we need is a demand that calls us to live a better life than we are currently living. But that call must come with compassion and grace, so that when we fail, we hear, "Father, forgive them, for they do not know what they are doing." This is exactly what I find in Jesus ... and that strikes me as a livable path, a yoke I can bear, a yoke that is in fact easier and lighter than any other option I have tried or heard of. Another ring of truth.

5. Jesus Is Powerfully Noncoercive

Jesus was known for speaking in parables, in stories that would yield meaning on many levels. If you wanted to stop at the surface level, you could. If you wanted to go deeper, you could. The point was always on the deeper level, but Jesus never forced the crowds to dig for it, and never threw it in their face. Thus his approach with the general public was remarkably subtle and nonconfrontational; it was gentle, not harsh; magnetic, not pushy; inviting, not driving ... an opportunity, not a threat. Take it or leave it. It's your choice. As he did with that successful young leader, he will watch you walk away if you choose — no lectures, no getting in the last word.

A few lines from one of the ancient prophets (Isaiah) seemed to fit him perfectly: He wouldn't be heard yelling in the streets. He wouldn't snuff out a dimly burning candle. He wouldn't break a bruised reed. No, his approach would be gentle, like a shepherd carrying a lamb in his arms ... not driving it, not whacking it, not threatening it ... gently carrying it along.

And that approach makes perfect sense in the development of a faith that is real. It has to be free and unforced, a choice rather than a necessity.

A Triple Fork

And that is how it has been for me. I didn't have to choose this path of faith. It came as a fork in the road—actually, a triple fork. One road represented following my typical adolescent urges. A second represented conforming to and complying with the calm and conservative rhythms of my religious heritage. Then there was a third path, a narrow, winding, uphill path leading off into the unknown, with Jesus' footprints in the dust. Here is how the choice happened for me.

As I have said, I grew up going to church, very conservative to be sure, but in many ways a good church nonetheless with sincere people who loved God and for the most part, each other too. At church and at home, I learned the Bible stories and learned to pray, and I cared about doing good and pleasing God.

But in my early teens, I did what a lot of kids my age do: I began to have my doubts. As I have explained, my religious heritage told me that evolution was a complete lie, that the earth had been created in six literal days some six thousand years ago. I had trouble with that in light of the growing evidence to the contrary. Furthermore, my church told me that we were among the very few who really worshiped God in his appointed way, but I found us to be not much if any better than other people I knew. So, although I had no one to talk with about these questions, in my heart I wondered. And I was afraid, because I thought I wasn't supposed to question or wonder or doubt.

About this time, I was invited to join a little rock and roll band ... and everybody knew that was sinful. To my parents' chagrin, I joined, and we played at teen club dances and bar mitzvahs and parties, at which at least some of what went on was also ... sinful. But all the same, to me, it was fun and exciting and free. I felt alive to be playing my saxophone, banging a tambourine, learning to dance. And I wondered, "If this stuff about God is true, then maybe I am in danger of getting into trouble here. But if it's not true, then who cares? Why shouldn't I have a good time?" In that simple line of thinking, for the first time it mattered to me whether I believed "this stuff about God" to be true or not. I realized my decision would take me down two very different paths.

I grew my hair long (another no-no), grew a scruffy adolescent beard (a clear sign of rebellion), wore faded blue jeans at all times (an apostate fabric if ever there was one), and vehemently drew attention to every hypocrisy I could find in the church (with a degree of maturity that matched my scruffy beard). And I am sure that many people who knew me at this time thought, "Oh, there he goes. Losing his faith."

Cognitive Dissonance

But the truth was, I was actually finding my faith. Yes, I was in a sense losing the faith that my parents and church had tried to give me. But this was necessary, because I had to find a faith with my own name on it, not just theirs. I guess psychologists would call this cognitive dissonance—that I had two conflicting value systems at work in my mind. But that cognitive dissonance created for me for the first time a fork in the road, one path being the attractive option that, if I wanted, I could drop faith altogether and "have a good time" like so many of my peers, without worrying about God and right and wrong and morality and all that.

Perhaps you see my dilemma. I was now presented with two unacceptable alternatives: Conform to my heritage and deny my doubts, or conform to my peers and deny my spiritual search.

A couple of things happened at this time, opening a third option for me. First, a fellow at my church invited me to join a Bible study group he had formed. Dave Miller was in college, a few years older than me, and at first, frankly, I didn't like him all that much. I was working hard on being a hippie, and he was a clean-cut, all-American athlete type. But he was persistent. He would drive forty-five minutes out of his way to pick me up for this Bible study group, and so I obliged him and went.

In that study group, the three or four other guys talked about their faith in a way I had never seen before. They related God and faith to their daily lives, to their struggles, to their fun, to their friendships, to their future plans, even to their sexuality. And it wasn't all about guilt and rules; it had more of the air of an adventure they were on with God ... an adventure with joy and reality and purpose.

Something else happened about this time. Largely because of this group, I started reading the Bible on my own. And I was fascinated. Sure, there were boatloads of things I didn't understand, and actually, quite a few I didn't agree with. But this Jesus, he fascinated me. He was magnetic to me.

More Contacts

About this time, I volunteered to be a counselor-in-training at a summer camp, and one of the other young counselors and

I would stay up late at night talking after the kids in our cabins were asleep. We talked about life, girls, God, music, faith. This fellow, Tom, had been deeply into drugs—pot, mescaline, maybe some LSD too. Some months earlier, he had opened his heart to Jesus, he said, and his life had changed. He had little or no church background, but it was clear to me that the same spirit that I sensed in Jesus as I read the Bible was also in this guy, the same spirit I had sensed in Dave's Bible study group, something alive, genuine, purposeful, free, kind ... something I didn't quite have yet, but maybe was starting to wish I had.

At summer's end, back at school, I got to know another guy. This guy had been one of the main marijuana dealers at my school, but now he was telling everybody that he had changed. And he had. As in the others, I sensed in him that special spirit, that special vitality I could read between the lines in the Gospels. Through him I met more people who, for all their faults, seemed to have this same spirit too.

The question for me was, which way was I going to go? Several months passed with that tug-of-war going on inside me. At first I was eighty-percent no, and twenty-percent yes; then it was fifty/fifty for a while, and eventually, the yes part overshadowed the no part, and I found that the spirit I had sensed in these other guys was now growing in me.

On a Maryland Hillside

One decisive experience occurred about this time. I seldom talk about this, because talking about some things tends to cheapen them, but this seems like an appropriate time to mention it. I was invited by one of my best friends to attend his church's youth retreat. I don't think I had ever been on a retreat before, as our denomination didn't have retreats. We went to a ramshackle retreat center somewhere in the Maryland hills, and had the usual round of silly get-acquainted games, camp food, and talks by the pastor and his guest speakers. The first night, I was somewhat surprised to lie in the dark of the cabin and hear the other boys start telling dirty jokes. I wasn't above telling some myself, but I remember thinking that among church kids, this probably shouldn't be happening.

The second day, things went along alright until the afternoon. Midway through the afternoon, we were sent off for a time of silence and solitude. The idea was to get alone somewhere and talk to God. I found a tree along a path, and figured that climbing it and sitting among the branches would be a good place to get close to God. It wasn't much of a spiritual experience. First, I couldn't get comfortable. The bark was rough, and my butt hurt. Second, ants were crawling up and down the trunk, and I became a part of their roadway. Then the mosquitoes started biting. I would get out a sentence of prayer, and then would shift my weight, flick off an ant, and scratch my newest mosquito bite. I would try to pray again, but would soon wonder, "When is that bell going to ring telling us this time is over?"

At some point though, I distinctly remember praying this prayer: "God, I want to stop fighting you. I want to be one hundred percent committed to you. I want to surrender to you. I want to say yes to you. I only ask one thing. Before I die, please allow me to see the most beautiful sights in the world, and hear the most beautiful sounds in the world, and feel the most beautiful experiences in the world." (Obviously, "beautiful" was an important word to this adolescent fledgling musician/hippie/spiritual seeker.)

Rough Bark, Ants, Mosquitoes, and Stars

No lightning bolts or visions of angels ensued. Eventually, I surrendered to the bark, the ants, and the mosquitoes and left the tree and ambled back to the mess hall for supper. The evening brought more harmless if not inane camp games and songs, and we were about to go to bed for another round, I supposed, of dirty jokes. But a few friends and I decided to take a detour and look at the stars. It was a clear, dry, high-pressure-system night, and the stars were glorious. I went off by myself, a stone's throw away from my buddies on that grassy round hill, and I lay back in the grass and gazed. And a thought, or series of thoughts, came to me with a power that now brings tears to my eyes as I recall it. I felt loved. The thoughts went like this: "Those stars are glorious, but I am more precious to God than a star. God didn't send Jesus into the world for stars, but for me. The God who made stars and galaxies and space and time sees me lying here on this hump of dirt and grass, and he loves me. I am loved."

Beautiful Things

And with that realization, I started to laugh. It wasn't funny, exactly; it was joy. It was a pure joy that I have experienced on a few occasions in my life, but only a few, and it was so intense it almost hurt after a while. I remember almost asking God to stop it, because I was becoming afraid; I thought I was about to break or burst, unable to contain such joy and light in my soul. And then I began to cry.

My friends were talking intently to one another all during this, opening up in that wonderful way that young people do and older people should do. Apparently they didn't hear me quietly laughing and crying. When my intense feelings began to subside,

I could again hear their voices through the silence, and I heard one of my friends say to another, and then to all the others, "I love you. I love all of you." And hearing that, I began to cry again.

More happened that night, but I don't need to go into it all. At some point in the early hours of the next morning, though, I remembered my prayer of the afternoon before, and I thought, "Yes, God has already answered it." I had seen the most beautiful thing on earth—the glory of God shining through creation, making it ring like a struck bell, making it glow with wonder. And I had heard the most beautiful thing in life—human beings telling other human beings that they love one another. And I had felt the most beautiful feeling in life—to be loved, really loved, by a God who knows me—my secrets, my faults, my doubts, my wrongs, my shame, along with my strengths and dreams and hopes and gifts—simply to be known and loved.

The experience, of course, faded, and its memory fades a bit with each telling of the story, because gradually I seem to remember the telling, the story, more than the experience itself. But that's okay. Other experiences have come, like Willard's view of the sea, experiences that, in Wordsworth's words ("Tintern Abbey"), bring

> *A presence that disturbs me with the joy*
> *of elevated thoughts; a sense sublime*
> *Of something far more deeply interfused,*
> *Whose dwelling is the light of setting suns,*
> *And the round ocean and the living air,*
> *And the blue sky, and in the mind of man;*
> *A motion and a spirit, that impels*
> *All thinking things, all objects of all thought,*
> *And rolls through all things.*

The fact remains that it is twenty-five years later, and I am still on that same path, learning to open my heart in new ways, savoring the same beauty, desiring that same spirit (or Spirit) of joy and love to fill me. I certainly have my ups and downs, and quite often that old "no" part of me stages a pretty strong counteroffensive. But the new spiritual "yes" seems to prove itself stronger than the old "no," and so I press on in this path, step by step, breath by breath.

And for this leg of the journey, I have felt that spirit prompting me to try to help you, across these pages, to find the path for yourself, so you can learn, in your own way and in your own time, how to say to God that one, life-changing word, yes.

Your Response

1. What one thing would you want to ask of God?
2. What yesses and nos are at work in your own life?
3. Is there any compelling reason for you not to say a wholehearted yes to God right now?
4. The most important things I have learned from this book are:
5. The most important things I want to do next are:
6. The people I would most like to dialogue with regarding spiritual matters are:

Resources

As a reader of *Finding Faith*, you are warmly invited to participate in the Finding Faith website on the internet, at www.crcc.org. Your comments and questions are welcome there too.

Consider getting away on a retreat of your own, either with a group or in solitude, to reflect on what you have learned so far in your spiritual search and to simply talk to God about it all. If you would like to organize a spiritual retreat for spiritual seekers in your area, please contact the Finding Faith website for referrals to trained retreat leaders.

Prayer

If a relationship with you could be compared to a home, and you were inviting me to come home to be part of your family, I would say yes. If it could be compared to a romance, and you were proposing a relationship of love and loyalty to me, again, I would say yes. If a relationship with you could be compared to a journey, and you were inviting me to follow you, I would say an enthusiastic yes. If a relationship with you could be compared to a school or a cause where you invite me to learn or work with you, I would say yes, yes, yes. I want my heart to be full of yes for you, God! I would like to express more of my feelings and desires and gratitude to you, God … (Continue in your own words.)

Afterword

It was about eight years ago that I began writing the first version of *Finding Faith*. Of everything I have written before and since, this book (along with *The Story We Find Ourselves In*) has a special place in my heart. The main reason for that special attachment has to do with my own sense of vocation in life.

Growing up, I never planned to be a pastor or author. For a while I dreamed of being a cartoonist, but there was one problem: I couldn't draw very well. My love of nature interested me in forestry for a while, or maybe wildlife management. In high school, inspired by a couple of great English teachers, I decided to become a high school teacher, and then in college, my dream morphed into being a college English professor. As my own faith and commitment grew, I never thought, "I should be a pastor." I thought, "I should live out my faith to my students and fellow faculty members in a secular university campus."

During the years I taught at the college level, I loved my work and had a deep sense of vocation in it. When I left higher education and became a pastor and spiritual leader (which some might say is an even higher form of education), I never felt I was more "holy" or "called" than I felt back in my university days. It was just a different way of living out the same calling.

And that calling, simply put, is what this book and its companion volume have been about: trying to help people find *good faith*—a faith that is real, an honest and intelligent faith that makes sense, a faith they can feel, a faith that moves them to become better people who help make a better world.

When you really care about something, you are never satisfied. You always wish you could do better. That is how I feel now. I am grateful for the chance to rework *Finding Faith* into two shorter and more focused volumes — the second of which you are now finishing. I am hopeful that both books will help you in your search for good faith and all it entails. But I also wish I could have done better.

But perhaps that is my act of faith: having done what little I could, to trust that God will take it and make it useful to people like you, people who are seeking for faith, people who are seeking God ... people whom, at this very moment, God is seeking too. May each be found by the other.

Sources and Resources

Bloom, Anthony. *Beginning to Pray*. Mahwah, NJ: Paulist Press, 1970.

Dillard, Annie. *Pilgrim at Tinker Creek*. New York: HarperCollins, 1988.

Guardini, Romano. *The Lord*. Washington, DC: Regnery, 1996.

King, Larry, with Rabbi Irwin Katsof. *Powerful Prayers: Conversations on Faith, Hope, and the Human Spirit with Today's Most Provocative People*. New York: St. Martin's Press/Renaissance Books, 1998.

Kreeft, Peter. *Making Sense Out of Suffering*. Ann Arbor, MI: Servant, 1986.

Kushner, Harold. *When Bad Things Happen to Good People*. New York: Avon, 1981.

Lewis, C. S. *The Problem of Pain*. New York: Macmillan, 1962.

McLaren, Brian. *The Church on the Other Side: Exploring the Radical Future of the Local Congregation*. Grand Rapids: Zondervan, 2000.

_____. *A Generous Orthodoxy*. Grand Rapids: Zondervan, 2004.

_____. *The Secret Message of Jesus: Uncovering the Truth That Could Change Everything*. Nashville: W Publishing, 2006.

_____. *The Story We Find Ourselves In*. San Francisco: Jossey-Bass, 2002.

Norris, Kathleen. *Amazing Grace: A Vocabulary of Faith*. New York: Riverhead, 1998.

Nouwen, Henri. *Life of the Beloved: Spiritual Living in a Secular World*. New York: Crossroad, 1996.

_____. *The Return of the Prodigal Son*. New York: Doubleday, 1994.

Oden, Thomas. *The Living God: Systematic Theology: Volume 1*. San Francisco: HarperSanFrancisco, 1992.

Peck, M. Scott. *The Road Less Traveled*. 1978. Reprint, New York: Simon & Schuster/Touchstone, 2003.

Pelikan, Jaroslav. *Jesus through the Centuries: His Place in the History of Culture*. 1985. Reprint, New Haven, CT: Yale University Press, 1999.

Polkinghorne, John C. *The Faith of a Physicist: Reflections of a Bottoms-Up Thinker*. Minneapolis: Augsburg Fortress, 1996.

Smith, Huston. *Beyond the Post-Modern Mind: The Place of Meaning in a Global Civilization*. Third edition. Wheaton, IL: Quest Books, 2003.

_____. *The World's Religions: Our Great Wisdom Traditions*. Reprint, San Francisco: HarperSanFrancisco, 1991.

Strobel, Lee. *The Case for Christ*. Grand Rapids: Zondervan, 1998.

Sweet, Leonard I. *Quantum Spirituality: A Postmodern Apologetic*. Dayton, OH: United Theological Seminary, 1991.

Tada, Joni Eareckson. *Joni*. Grand Rapids: Zondervan, 1976.

Tolkien, J. R. R. *Return of the King*. Lord of the Rings, Part 3. 1956. Reprint, Boston: Houghton Mifflin, 1999.

Tolstoy, Leo. *A Confession*. 1879. Reprint, *A Confession and Other Religious Writings*. New York: Norton, 1983.

Tournier, Paul. *The Adventure of Living*. 1965. Reprint, New York: Harper & Row, 1979.

Willard, Dallas. *The Divine Conspiracy*. San Francisco: HarperSanFrancisco, 1998.

Winner, Lauren. *Mudhouse Sabbath*. Mahwah, NJ: Paraclete, 2003.

Yancey, Philip. *Disappointment with God*. Grand Rapids: Zondervan, 1988.

_____. *The Jesus I Never Knew*. Grand Rapids: Zondervan, 1995.

_____. *What's So Amazing About Grace*. Grand Rapids: Zondervan, 1997.

_____. *Where Is God When It Hurts?* Grand Rapids: Zondervan, 1977.